Learning for Themselves

Pathways to independence in the classroom

JENI WILSON & KATH MURDOCH

 Routledge
Taylor & Francis Group

LONDON AND NEW YORK

First published 2008
by Curriculum Corporation
PO Box 177 Carlton South Vic 3050 Australia

This version published 2009
by Routledge
2 Park Square, Milton Park, Abingdon, Oxon OX14 4RN

Simultaneously published in the USA and Canada
by Routledge
711 Third Avenue, New York, NY 10017

Routledge is an imprint of the Taylor & Francis Group, an informa business

British Library Cataloguing in Publication Data
A catalogue record for this book is available from the British Library

Library of Congress Cataloging in Publication Data
Wilson, Jeni.
Learning for themselves : pathways for thinking and independent learning in
the primary classroom / Jeni Wilson and Kath Murdoch.
p. cm.
Includes bibliographical references.
1. Independent study. 2. Education, Elementary. 3. Thought and thinking–Study
and teaching (Elementary) I. Murdoch, Kath. II. Title.
LB1049.W558 2009
372.139′43–dc22   2008039938

ISBN13: 978–0–415–48699–6 (pbk)

Contents

Acknowledgements

We have been fortunate to have worked with many teachers and students over the last decade and the ideas in this book have developed as a result of these experiences. Some of the frameworks in this book are based on ideas developed in collaboration with teachers who have specific needs and students in mind. Others have been developed and trialled in a range of classrooms by us and our colleagues in schools.

We hope you enjoy implementing the ideas in your own classroom. But our biggest hope is that these frameworks will inspire you to be independent and innovative and to create your own structures with and for your students.

We thank the teachers and students from the following schools for allowing us to share their work and the work we have developed with them:

St Albans East Primary School

Killara Primary School

Sunshine Primary School

Brunswick South West Primary School

Roberts McCubbin Primary School

Hawthorn West Primary School

Grimwade House

Elsternwick Primary School

Special thanks to Kim Wise from Brunswick South West Primary School for giving us very useful feedback on the manuscript.

Dedication

This book is dedicated to my mother, Margaret and my parents-in-law, Margaret and George, whose collective wisdom and compassion has taught me much about nurturing independence in children. (KM)

For my boys, Ethan, Madison and Stephen, as always. (JW)

Introduction

If I am always the one to think of where to go next

If where we go is always the decision of the curriculum or my curiosity and not theirs

If motivation is mine

If I always decide on the topic to be studied, the title of the story,

the problem to be worked on

If I am always the one who has reviewed their work and decided what they need

How will they ever know how to begin?

From *The Things We Steal from Children* by Dr John Edwards
and Sandra Russell (1999)

Ask most teachers what they believe to be a key goal of their work and they will often reply that it is to help students become effective, independent learners. In contrast to traditional classroom practices where students were dependent on the teacher to make decisions about their learning, classrooms are increasingly viewed as places in which students 'learn to learn'. As we grow in our understanding of effective pedagogy, we are also recognising the need for more small group and one-on-one teaching opportunities. For this to happen effectively, we must develop students' capacity to work independently and manage themselves as learners. This awareness leads to students who are more conscious of what they do and do not understand, who are able to set goals, identify their needs and monitor their learning. Being able to manage their own learning, thinking and behaviour is critical in the development of individuals who can successfully navigate their way through a world of rapidly changing knowledge and the demands for new and transferable skills.

We believe that students will only develop the skills and behaviours for effective, independent learning if they are given opportunities to be independent. This requires teachers to have a repertoire of effective strategies and structures – but it also requires teachers who view students as increasingly capable of managing their learning and who are willing to share the power of teaching and learning with their students. Sharing power is also about being explicit and transparent about our purposes. It involves direct and clear instruction about how to 'do learning'. Through clear explanation and reflection, issues such as how to stay motivated, how to organise resources, how to solve problems, how to set and work towards manageable goals become part of the accepted discourse in the classroom. Classrooms that foster independence are places where there is much shared discussion about thinking and learning.

Another key to fostering independence in the classroom is to recognise the *differences* among individuals and to develop ways to cater for these differences. Often referred to as a 'differentiated' approach, classrooms in which students are regularly given choices about what and how they will learn, and are involved in setting goals and assessing their own learning, are classrooms in which independent learning is more likely to emerge.

Independence is not about creating a 'teacher free' context. On the contrary – the teacher plays a critical role in guiding, supporting and critiquing students *as* they work through these tasks.

There are many ways in which teachers provide opportunities for effective student learning. These include: teacher modelling and demonstration, whole class and small group experiences, and the use of specific teaching procedures and strategies. Effective teachers use a wide range of approaches to meet the needs of their students. The specific emphasis of this book is the provision of frameworks for independent learning. The following principles underpin these frameworks and provide a rationale for why it is so important to nurture opportunities for students to learn for themselves.

Principles of independent learning

- All students can learn – but each student will be motivated to learn in different ways.

- Each student has unique learning preferences. Students do not all learn in the same way.

- When students are given choice, responsibility and ownership, they are more engaged, motivated and productive.

- Students learn at different rates. Either rushing or delaying students' progress can reduce engagement and impact negatively on learning outcomes.

- When students are given more responsibility for their learning, they are often in a better position to develop essential skills in thinking, research, communication and self-management.

- Not all students need to be 'doing the same thing' at the same time. Classrooms are, increasingly, places where small groups and individuals are pursuing a diversity of tasks.

- When students feel valued for who they are and what they bring to the learning environment, they are more likely to engage confidently in the learning process.

- When students achieve success because they can manage and enjoy the tasks, their confidence to tackle other independent tasks is increased.

- When the stress of comparative assessment is reduced, students are more likely to take risks in their learning and feel comfortable to set themselves goals.

- The appropriate level of challenge is important for motivation. The teacher's role in determining and monitoring this is important for facilitating learning during independent tasks. (In other words, independent learning is not just a matter of providing great tasks and hoping for the best.)

- Teachers have a vital role in nurturing independent learners. Importantly teachers must take responsibility for helping to define content and skills for students to work towards.

Summary of independent learning tasks

Pathway	Curriculum area	Focus question	Task
Learning preferences	Society & environment	*How do natural disasters affect us?*	Three level ladder
Learning preferences	Society & environment	*Why do people immigrate to the UK?*	It all adds up
Learning preferences	Society & environment	*What are wetlands? Why are they important?*	The artist's choice
Thinking dispositions	Society & environment	*How did* Charlotte's Web *make me think?*	Thinking in different ways
Thinking	Society & environment	*How can we live more sustainably?*	Thinking graphically
Inquiry	Society & environment	*What makes your community special?*	Resource detective
Inquiry	Society & environment	*How has the UK changed?*	Now I understand
Personal challenges	Society & environment	*How can we use water more wisely?*	Personal, local, global
Personal challenges	Society & environment	*What makes a good leader?*	A self-assessment matrix
Inquiry	Society & environment	*What does it mean to take on a challenge?*	Voices of the people
Learning preferences	Health & wellbeing	*How can we keep ourselves safe at home and at school?*	Choose it, make it!
Learning preferences	Health & wellbeing	*How can I help someone?*	Think, do, feel
Learning preferences	Health & wellbeing	*How do we entertain ourselves?*	What's your style?
Thinking	Health & wellbeing	*What is a safe risk?*	The coloured thinking hats
Thinking	Health & wellbeing	*How do I learn?*	The thinking gears
Thinking	Health & wellbeing	*How does advertising affect us?*	The six thinking hats
Thinking	Health & wellbeing	*How do I make decisions?*	Tic tac toe
Thinking	Health & wellbeing	*What do I think about thinking?*	Mix and match
Thinking	Health & wellbeing	*What did I learn this term?*	Thinking over it
Personal challenges	Health & wellbeing	*How can I keep myself healthy?*	Targetted learning
Personal challenges	Health & wellbeing	*How can we form respectful relationships?*	Challenge climb
Inquiry	Health & wellbeing	*How can we create a healthy community?*	Question matrix
Learning preferences	Science & technology	*How do we measure weather?*	See, hear, do
Thinking	Science & technology	*What makes a good structure?*	Bloom's activity choices
Thinking	Science & technology	*What can we change?*	The thinker's keys
Inquiry	Science & technology	*What can I learn about spiders?*	Data chart
Inquiry	Science & technology	*How do animals survive in their environment?*	Must do, can do
Personal challenges	Science & technology	*How can I make a toy with moving parts?*	Think, plan, do
Learning preferences	Science & technology	*How are plants and animals the same? How are they different?*	Choose your own adventure
Thinking	Science & technology	*What is an inventor?*	Using the thinker's keys
Inquiry			My passion project
Personal challenges			Personal best project

Chapter 1

Making it happen in the classroom

When we adults think of children there is a simple truth that we ignore: childhood is not preparation for life; childhood is life. A child isn't getting ready to live; a child is living. No child will miss the zest and joy of living unless these are denied by adults who have convinced themselves that childhood is a period of preparation. How much heartache we would save ourselves if we would recognise children as partners with adults in the process of living, rather than always viewing them as apprentices. How much we could teach each other; we have the experience and they have the freshness. How full both our lives could be.

John A Taylor (1991)

This book offers teachers a varied selection of frameworks intended to allow students *choice* and *voice* within a structure for responsible, independent learning. The frameworks provided do not, in themselves, teach students how to work independently. But in conjunction with the right kind of classroom culture and organisation they help build student capacity for independence.

The chapters are organised under four broad areas: thinking, learning preferences, inquiry and personal challenges. The learning task proformas presented within each chapter are designed to support students in working independently through an activity or sequence of activities. Most tasks have been designed using content drawn from commonly addressed topics in primary school curriculums and they vary in their degree of challenge. At the beginning of each chapter, a table is provided to indicate the approximate level for which each task is designed. Most can be adjusted to suit older or younger age groups. Many of these tasks were developed to provide a more differentiated avenue for learning once students had explored a topic together for a while.

It is anticipated that teachers will be able to use these tasks as part of a broader unit of work that explores similar or related content. Some of them have also been used as the basis for homework tasks.

The learning tasks consist of two proformas: one that provides a focus question and one that does not. These modified proformas offer opportunities for teachers and students to use and adapt the structures to create their own learning tasks to suit their particular teaching and learning goals. All learning task proformas are provided in the Appendix.

The learning tasks are designed for individual students or small group use. They are structured to allow students to decide what they will attempt to do, how they might go about it and, often, how they will present their learning. By providing students with these choices, we help them come to understand more about themselves as learners. In general, the tasks share several common features:

- students can make **choices** about what they will do
- there are **guidelines and parameters** to help students make wise choices and to help them manage their learning
- suggested activities are **open-ended** and allow for multiple outcomes
- frameworks are generally '**integrative**' in nature, working across the curriculum
- there is a focus on **higher order thinking**
- most tasks are accompanied by some form of **self-assessment**
- tasks are designed to develop **skills** as well as **understandings**.

In using these learning tasks with students, it is very important that teachers do not simply 'hand them out' and expect students to be able to manage them without support and guidance. We suggest teachers:

- **model** an example to the students (for example, enlarge a task to A3 size and show students how it could be approached, or model it on a board)
- discuss possible **assessment criteria** that could accompany the task so students are aware of your expectations
- hold regular, small group **conferences** so you can keep track of how students are approaching the task and the degree to which they are coping with its demands (there are proformas to accompany such conferences in the support materials section in the Appendix)
- **identify** the skills and processes the students will need to complete the tasks and ensure that they are adequately supported in the development of those skills.

Effective implementation of these 'independent' learning tasks requires some examination of three core elements: the skills and qualities of independent learners; the beliefs, behaviours and skills of teachers; and the nature of the tasks themselves. These aspects are discussed as follows.

What is an independent learner?

Working independently involves thinking, feeling, and doing. Independent learners know and feel they can make responsible choices and decisions and they get the job done.

As self-motivators, independent learners:

- are eager and curious
- are proactive and willing to take risks
- are able to set goals and initiate tasks with less direction
- know that positive thinking is useful
- are likely to produce work beyond expectations, particularly when self initiated
- enjoy a challenge.

As self-managers, independent learners:

- are thoughtful and deliberate in their actions
- persevere despite distractions
- avoid procrastination, and need minimal reminders and prompts to reach their goals
- draw upon a range of ways of thinking to get complex tasks completed
- make plans and set goals using a range of systems to develop routines and organise themselves, their materials and their time
- attempt to sort through problems first before consulting others.

As self-appraisers, independent learners:

- are self aware and can articulate their needs and strengths as a learner
- take time to reflect on effective learning strategies
- use their own judgements to choose appropriate strategies and actions
- use positive self talk and other ways to motivate and praise themselves
- do not constantly seek approval or guidance from others
- can adapt more readily to change in routines and expectations
- ask questions to clarify their understanding of given tasks and readily act upon feedback.

What skills do independent learners have?

Questioning

Independent learners ask a range of questions to find out more, make connections, clarify, challenge, improve their understandings, and to identify 'big issues'. Their questions go well beyond the managerial, for example: What do I need to do? How do I do...? They test opinions, question ideas, the learning process and their own progress.

Reflection and metacognition

Independent learners take time to think about their work, ideas and thinking. When thinking reflectively, they engage in active, persistent, systematic and careful consideration of ideas for a deeper understanding or to resolve states of doubt, a question, or a perplexing issue. When thinking metacognitively, the more independent learner is able to reflect and draw upon their existing knowledge and on their thought processes (including feelings). They can identify where they are in the learning process or in the process of solving a problem, their content-specific knowledge, and their knowledge about their personal learning or problem-solving strategies. They are aware of what they know, of what needs to be done, what has been done and what might be done in particular learning contexts. They can evaluate their ongoing knowledge and mental processes in progress. They can make judgements about their own thinking processes, knowledge, capacities and limitations.

Organisation

Independent learners develop systems for planning, organising and managing tasks to optimise progress towards their goals. They think about how they will manage their materials, time and themselves to get the job done. They pay attention to process and task completion.

Identifying, gathering and critiquing resources

Independent learners systematically, thoughtfully and selectively gather and appraise beyond the obvious. They check sources and evidence of validity/relevance, will challenge texts, compare information and make connections among ideas.

Risk-taking and resilience

Independent learners are inquisitive and approach new situations without fear of failure. They do not avoid challenges. They enjoy a challenge and do not opt for the same approach each time. They are confident enough to try something new and design or try creative ways of doing things. They are also comfortable if what they try does not work. They do not get overly 'bogged down' when something is not working and are willing to change their own point of view and way of working. These students cope with change readily and often 'multi-task'. They are flexible, innovative and will consider different solutions. They can 'go with the flow', changing their thinking and actions depending on what is required.

Seeking and accepting feedback

Independent learners are open to new ideas, listen to and take advice, because they understand that this is likely to improve their learning and results. They will seek feedback (from peers, teachers and others) to clarify requirements, improve their performance and assist progress. This is different from continually 'checking in' with the teacher.

How can teachers nurture independence in their students?

Although it may seem contradictory, the tasks, skills and qualities presented in this book are not about creating a 'teacher free' environment where students manage all of their learning and require little or no support from the teacher! Ultimately, our goal is to help students come to understand who they are as learners, their particular strengths and needs, and to develop within them the capacity to learn continuously and actively. We want students who know how to take responsibility for themselves as learners and who delight in that challenge. *All this happens only with the support of a strategic and highly interactive teacher.*

In the classrooms where we see students working most effectively and independently, we find teachers who have, above all else, a strong sense of *purpose* behind all they do. These teachers know why they are doing what they are doing and, importantly, they make that very explicit to their students. Teachers apprentice students into learning by 'letting them in on the secret' – they make transparent the processes and skills needed to achieve a desired outcome. They spotlight *how* the learning is taking place as well as what learning is taking place.

These purposeful and explicit teachers are also keenly aware of the individual differences among their students. They take time to gather data about the needs of individuals and offer tasks that are open-ended enough to cater for that variety. Once they have that real knowledge of individuals, they are better placed to help them realise their potential for independence. Different students, of course, require different levels of support. A teacher who is passionate about helping his or her students become effective learners quickly learns where to place the 'scaffolding' for certain students, and when to remove some of the layers of that scaffold. The support materials provided on the CD-ROM offer many structures that assist teachers in providing the guidance and organisation necessary for the effective implementation of the independent learning tasks.

In the day-to-day practical running of the classroom, teachers can help support independent work by:

- establishing clear rules and routines
- ensuring that students are clear about the requirements of the task, the due date, and checking in with them regularly
- conferencing with individuals or small groups to check progress (there are record sheets in the support materials section in the Appendix)
- discussing time management techniques, effective work habits and rules of courtesy
- checking internet resources for suitability
- running targeted 'skills' workshops to develop students' capacity in certain areas such as note-taking, summarising, organising notes
- regularly checking student record keeping, for example work diaries and completion sheets
- making time for feedback, sharing and celebrating achievements.

Frequently asked questions

How do the independent learning tasks relate to inquiry learning?

Many teachers favour an inquiry approach to the design and implementation of curriculum. Developing the skills and qualities for more independent learning complement this approach – indeed, the inquiry process itself is based on a view of the student as capable of asking and investigating questions of significance. Some of the frameworks in this book draw on the inquiry process (see Chapter 4) while other frameworks may be used by students as part of a broader unit of inquiry or within other curriculum structures. Nurturing independence is critical to success in inquiry learning so these learning tasks support the skills and qualities that characterise the inquiring classroom.

How do we fit this independent work in with everything else we have to cover?

The frameworks in this collection can be used to support existing curriculum content. We have selected examples based on commonly taught 'units' in primary and middle years. This has been a deliberate choice so that teachers can embed them within existing structures rather than using them in an isolated way. When students develop the skills to work more independently, teachers are able to work more efficiently and effectively on the expected curriculum as well as providing opportunities for students to negotiate aspects of their learning.

Teachers nurture independence when …	Teachers hinder the development of independence when …
They spend time investigating the learning interests and **preferences** of each student.	They favour one kind of learning style in their planning and teaching.
They spend time setting up a classroom environment where students feel comfortable to take **risks**.	Time spent on classroom environment is considered peripheral to core business.
Students are invited to **share** what they want to learn about and how they like to learn. Their ideas are used to **inform** curriculum planning and students are involved in **goal setting**.	Teachers make all the decisions about curriculum, largely based on levels specified by curriculum documents.
Teachers provide students with real opportunities for **choice** and **decision making**.	Teachers offer little or no choice to students about what or how they will learn.
There is regular, sustained **dialogue** among students. Questions are fostered and teachers are active listeners.	Teachers do most of the talking and questioning.
Learning routines favour **small group** and **one-on-one** teaching where students are highly involved.	Most teaching is conducted at the whole class level. Students are often passive recipients.
Students expect that they will work in **different groupings** for different purposes. Sometimes they choose these groups and sometimes groups are organised for them.	Teachers make all the decisions about who will work with whom.
Individuality is **celebrated** and students are encouraged to take reasonable risks.	Conformity is sought and reinforced.
Students have opportunities for sustained learning time – teachers show a **flexible approach** and allow more **time** when it is needed.	Timetables offer 'bite-sized' learning episodes that hinder a student's capacity to follow alternative pathways or pursue something in depth.
There is a clear and negotiated classroom **management plan**. Clear protocols for behaviour are consistently followed.	There is no clear behaviour management plan. Students are not involved in making decisions about expected behaviour or consequences.
Materials and resources are **shared**. Students have access to most resources and do not have to seek permission for everything they use.	Teachers are the 'gatekeeper' of all or most resources.
Students do not have a **fixed seat** in the room. They move around the room according to the demands of the activity.	Students always sit in the same place, usually specified by the teacher.
Student questions (including self-questioning), **reflective thinking** and metacognition are essential for students making their own decisions.	Little or no time is allowed for reflective practice.
Students are involved in setting goals and **self-assessing**.	Teachers determine learning goals for students without consultation. Students are not asked or expected to assess their own learning.

What about classroom management?

Many (but by no means all) management problems are due to poor student engagement. When students are given a 'voice' in their learning, they generally feel more valued and engaged. We have found that when teachers bring more choice and ownership into the way they work with students some management issues are resolved.

At the same time, we recognise that quality management is essential *for* independent learning. The two definitely 'feed' each other. Developing skills for independent learning is more possible in an environment where teachers use a positive, clear and constructive approach to classroom management. The way we manage our classrooms sends important messages to students. Authoritarian environments tell students that they are less capable of decision making and that they are not trusted to make choices. In classrooms that are too 'loose', chaotic and poorly managed, students often lack the important sense of security that routine and clear expectations provide. An effective learning environment relies on establishing shared core rules, routines and a discipline plan. William Glasser (1998) argues that classroom relationships (and, therefore learning) are enhanced when teachers attend to the five basic needs we all have for internal motivation: survival, love and belonging, power, freedom and fun.

What do we do about those children who just can't work independently?

We recognise that, for various reasons, some students present us with challenges that cannot be easily addressed even by the most fair and negotiated class discipline plan. Being a part of a constructive learning community brings with it responsibilities as well as rights. The right to be part of this community may need to be 'earned' by some students through individualised and targetted contracts or behaviour plans. These behaviour plans are one way we can begin to assist students to become more independent in their learning. Individual contracts allow students to have some ownership and control over the management of their behaviour.

Isn't this kind of work more appropriate for older students?

Spend any time in an open-ended, play-based preschool environment and you will quickly reassess the idea that young children cannot be independent! Both within the home and in preschool, children will exhibit an enormous capacity to make choices, to invent, to question, to sustain interest and to take initiative. Interestingly, we often observe older children being given far fewer choices and opportunities to be independent than their three- or four-year-old counterparts! *All* children have the capacity to think, learn and behave independently. Different children will require different levels of support at different times.

How do you resource this when children may be working on different topics at the same time?

Many of the learning tasks in this collection do not rely on one type of resource (for example, print-based). Instead, the tasks draw on a wide range of resources available within the school and the community. Because the focus of these tasks is independence, they are designed to encourage students to access resources for themselves and are, therefore, appropriately 'pitched' at primary school students.

What about learning to work together?

Although many of the tasks in this collection are geared towards individual students, they can often be adapted for use as a cooperative or team-based task. In any classroom, it is important to have a balance of tasks that require collaboration and those that may be carried out more individually. Some of the more 'sustained' tasks (such as the passion projects in Chapter 4) will be enhanced by organising small support groups where students share ideas and give feedback to each other. Being independent does not mean being isolated!

What about the home? What if parents don't value or foster independence?

As with all new approaches or innovations, it is important to explain the purpose of these tasks to parents. Most parents share the teacher's goal of helping their child learn to manage themselves, set goals, self-assess and self-motivate. When the tasks are explained with these broad purposes in mind, parents are more likely to understand and support their students in carrying them out. If these independent learning tasks are given as 'homework' it is particularly important that information about their purpose accompanies the task.

My style – Independent learning tasks

Task	Focus question / Area	Brief description	Year level
Three level ladder Multiple intelligences page 18	*How do **natural disasters** affect us?* Society & environment	Students choose among 15 activities and select three to collect, organise and represent information in different ways.	Upper
Choose it, make it! Multiple intelligences page 20	*How can we keep ourselves **safe** at home and at school?* Health & wellbeing	Students choose to create a poster, book, dance/movement, or model/construction to represent their ideas.	Lower
It all adds up Multiple intelligences page 22	*Why do people **immigrate** to the UK?* Society & environment	Students choose among eight activities, ranked by points, that require them to organise, investigate, compose, articulate, perform, write, create or persuade. They must achieve the value of six points.	Middle / Upper
Choose your own adventure Modalities page 24	*How are **plants** and **animals** the same? How are they different?* Science & technology	Students demonstrate their understandings by writing and drawing, making and doing, and saying or singing. They select, plan and justify their choices.	
See, hear, do Modalities page 26	*How do we measure **weather**?* Science & technology	Students show their understandings in three different ways: visual, auditory and kinesthetic. They also self-assess.	Lower
Think, do, feel Modalities page 28	*How can I **help someone**?* Health & wellbeing	Students respond to prompting questions to plan social action and reflect on feelings.	Lower
What's your style? Learning styles page 30	*How do we **entertain** ourselves?* Health & wellbeing	Students select from four sets of activities organised according to learning styles. They use the activity selected to demonstrate their understandings.	Middle / Upper
The artist's choice Learning preferences page 32	*What are **wetlands**? Why are they important?* Society & environment	Students are asked to be a painter, musician, photographer, sculptor, cartoonist, dancer or animator to show what they have learnt. They need to plan their work and justify their choices.	Upper

Support materials for independent learning tasks with a focus on learning preferences: 1 Keeping track of tasks; 3 Record of conversations with and observations of students; 4 My weekly diary; 5 My individual record sheet; 6 Free choice tickets and free choice tickets record sheet; 7 Creating independent learning tasks; 8 Ideas for developing independent activities; 9 Ideas for resourcing play-based learning centres; 10 Using modes: activity menus; 12 My contract; 18 Independent learner prompt cards; 19 Trouble shooting poster and cards; 20 Reminders for group work; 21 What kind of learner have I been today?; 22 Managing your time checklist; 23 My learning journal; 25 Head, hand and heart self-assessment; 26 Learning review lucky dip cards; 27 Self-assessment; 28 Pick-a-box self-assessment.

Chapter 2

My style
A focus on learning preferences

Student engagement is enhanced when students have opportunities to learn using different learning preferences. Giving students opportunities to seek, process and communicate in their preferred ways of learning provides an important avenue for independence. The emphasis in this chapter is on students making their own choices based on their own learning preferences.

Several theorists have attempted to explain differences among learning preferences, for example modalities, multiple intelligences and learning styles. Although some people use these words interchangeably, each provides a particular theoretical framework that can be used for planning and auditing learning experiences.

Most learning tasks in this chapter are clearly designed with a particular framework in mind. In some cases the framework may include learning preferences based on the work of more than one theorist. The tasks are contextualised in particular content (the particular focus is emboldened). A description of the tasks and approximate age suitability is also indicated as a guide.

Multiple Intelligences (Gardner, 1983)

Multiple Intelligences (MI) is a cognitive model. It is used to describe how students use their intelligences (abilities or capacities) to solve problems and create products. These intelligences can vary according to the context.

Intelligence	Description	Examples
Musical/Rhythmic	Communicates expressively through music, rhythm and performance.	Retell using music and movement Write a song or chant to explain
Verbal/Linguistic	Uses written and spoken language, for example to explain, convince, report, persuade, comprehend, express, humour, debate, collect and sort information.	Write a letter, wiki, email or blog
Bodily/Kinesthetic	Uses movement to express and represent ideas and feelings. Has a preference for hands-on activities, to manipulate, construct and fix things.	Perform a puppet play Complete a construction or props for a performance

Intelligence	Description	Examples
Visual/Spatial	Thinks visually, creates visual images, designs patterns/plans to graphically/ diagrammatically process and represent ideas.	Create a mind map Retell using key images
Naturalist	Recognises pattern and order in the natural world.	Find natural objects to represent/illustrate concepts
Logical/ Mathematical	Thinks inductively and deductively. Reasons, uses logical argument, prediction and hypotheses. Likes to work with numbers and abstract patterns, and can make connections.	Use a diagram to organise information Map or chart results
Interpersonal (group)	Considers issues from different perspectives and able to empathise with others. Prefers working with others.	Discuss ideas with others Give a team presentation
Intrapersonal (self)	Identifies own strengths and weaknesses and sets goals. Able to reflect on and ask questions about their thinking, learning, feelings and actions.	Record in a reflective journal Create an action plan
Existential	Poses and ponders questions about life and human existence. Can see the big picture, summarise and synthesise broad ideas.	Philosophical discussions

Learning styles (Gregorc-Butler, 1985)

The Gregorc-Butler learning styles indicate the approach people generally take to process information regardless of the content. The framework includes the following.

Concrete sequential	Concrete random
Hands-on experiential learning: ordered, logical processing. Example: organise a presentation, radio broadcast or flow chart	Hands-on experiential learning: can process information in a haphazard, non-linear fashion. Example: make a collage, design a brochure
Abstract sequential	**Abstract random**
Theoretical thinking beyond a particular example/context: ordered, logical processing. Example: design a slogan, write a proposal	Theoretical thinking beyond a particular example/context: can process information in a haphazard, non-linear fashion. Example: conduct interviews, role-play

Modalities

Modalities is primarily a sensory-based model which includes the modes (visual, auditory, kinesthetic) through which students both acquire information and demonstrate what they know.

Visual mode	Examples
Generally visual learners learn from what they see or observe (real life situations and other visuals). They may readily recall the content of written texts and may easily remember what they have written, drawn or observed. Visual learners often think in pictures. They tend to like details, problem-solving and planning.	Draw a story map Research statistics and find patterns Do a book/CD/web search Draw a cartoon strip Create a concept/mind map or other graphic organiser Retell as a cartoon using speech bubbles or as a board game Use a slide show to summarise key ideas Write a reflective journal
Auditory (oral / verbal) mode	**Examples**
Generally auditory learners enjoy and learn through listening (music, rhymes, debates) and speaking, but can be distracted by noises or sounds not directly related or relevant to what they are focussing on. They may talk to themselves and talk out problems through vocalising.	Make up a song or rap Make an audio or videotape Engage in a debate Conduct a chat show or current affairs show Write and read an acrostic poem Recite a created limerick Make sound effects Create a proverb or riddle Narrate a story
Kinesthetic (tactile) mode	**Examples**
Generally kinesthetic learners learn by hands-on experiences (touching, manipulating) and direct physical involvement rather than by being a passive observer. They enjoy performance, movement and action. They may communicate their experiences through body language. Kinesthetic learners more readily remember what they have done rather than what they have seen or heard.	Make simple devices/products, puzzle or card /board game Use construction materials or play dough to make a model Make a diorama Make a mobile Make a wall hanging Make shadow/stick/finger puppets to dramatise Make a frieze Write and enact a role-play or other performance

An extensive menu of activities for multi-modal learning is provided in the support materials in the Appendix.

Focus: How do natural disasters affect us?

Start at the bottom. Choose three activities, one from each row: one to **collect** information, one to **organise** information, one to **create** a product to show what you have learnt.

Learning preferences

Three level ladder

	Word	Mathematical	Visual	Musical	Tactile
3 Create	Write a disaster plan	Create a graph showing the trends or impact of disasters over time	Make a slide show of visual images	Create a piece of music, soundscape or song to describe an event or its impact	Show through freeze frame two possible responses to a natural disaster
2 Organise	Write the reflective diary entry of a victim for the week following a natural disaster	Create a timeline showing dates of natural disasters in a particular place/country over time	Create a diagram to show the consequences of a natural disaster on people and/or the environment	Select music that you believe best depicts feelings related to natural disasters	Sort objects used for preventing or responding to natural disasters. Use a graphic organiser, for example, a cluster diagram if useful
1 Collect	Collect newspaper articles about natural disasters	Find statistics about natural disasters on the internet	Use the internet to collect visual images about natural disasters	Find examples of music written to accompany film footage of natural disasters	Find objects or instruments that are associated with preventing or responding to natural disasters

Name: _____ Date: _____

Focus: _____

Start at the bottom. Create three activities, one for each row: one to **collect** information, one to **organise** information, one to **create** a product to show what you have learnt.

	Word	Mathematical	Visual	Musical	Tactile
3 Create					
2 Organise					
1 Collect					

Focus: How can we keep ourselves safe at home and at school?

Choose an activity. Choose how you will do it.

Design a poster

Create a poster to show other children how they can be safe at home or at school.

You could make your poster using:
- ★ paints ☐
- ★ pencils ☐
- ★ pastels ☐
- ★ crayons ☐
- ★ inks ☐
- ★ magazine pictures ☐
- ★ clip art from the computer ☐
- ★ photos ☐
- ★ collage ☐

Make a model

Use materials to make a model to teach other children about how to be safe at home or at school.

You could use:
- ★ Lego ☐
- ★ boxes ☐
- ★ play dough ☐
- ★ pipe cleaners ☐
- ★ blocks ☐
- ★ other found objects ☐

Use dance/movement

Use your body to help other children learn about how to be safe at home or at school.

You could:
- ★ find a song about keeping safe and make up actions to it ☐
- ★ make up a safety song with actions ☐
- ★ dance or move to music to show how to be safe ☐
- ★ use freeze frames to show people acting unsafely and safely ☐
- ★ make up a play to show how to keep safe ☐

Write a book

Write a little book (approximately eight pages long) to explain to other children why and how they can be safe at home or at school.

You could write:
- ★ a true story about yourself ☐
- ★ a pretend story with a message ☐
- ★ an instruction book ☐
- ★ a fact book ☐

Learning preferences

Choose it, make it!

Name: _____ Date: _____

Focus: _____

Choose an activity. Choose how you will do it.

Design a poster

You could make your poster using:

* paints ☐
* pencils ☐
* pastels ☐
* crayons ☐
* inks ☐
* magazine pictures ☐
* clip art from the computer ☐
* photos ☐
* collage ☐

Make a model

You could use:

* Lego ☐
* boxes ☐
* play dough ☐
* pipe cleaners ☐
* blocks ☐
* other found objects ☐

Use dance/movement

You could:

* find a song and make up actions ☐
* make up a song with actions ☐
* dance or move to music ☐
* use freeze frames ☐
* make up a play ☐

Write a book

You could write:

* a true story ☐
* a pretend story with a message ☐
* an instruction book ☐
* a fact book ☐

Learning preferences

It all adds up

Focus: Why do people immigrate to the UK?

Make a selection of tasks to the value of six points.

Organise!

Find out about the history of immigration in the UK. Show significant events on a timeline.

Value 2 points ☐

Investigate!

Use the Office of National Statistics website (www.statistics.gov.uk) to find out about patterns of immigration. Show and explain some of these patterns on a graph.

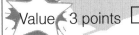

Value 3 points ☐

Compose!

Listen to some songs that describe the experiences of people who have come to the UK from other countries. Using what you know about the stories of immigrants, create your own song or piece of music to describe the experience to others.

Value 3 points ☐

Articulate!

You are the Minister for Immigration and have to prepare a speech titled: 'Why immigration is important to the UK'. Include the social and economic benefits. Refer to information from the Home Office and other sources.

Value 1 point ☐

Perform!

Using information you have gathered about the story of one or more immigrants, role-play the story as if it were your own. Consider using props/costumes to accompany your performance.

Value 2 points ☐

Create!

Find some photos or images that describe what it is like to migrate to the UK. Create your own visual image (painting, photo, collage, drawing) to show what the immigration experience is like.

Value 3 points ☐

Write!

Imagine you are an immigrant to the UK in the early–mid 1800's, 1900s or 2000s. Write a letter to your family describing your experiences and feelings. You may create this as a postcard.

Value 1 point ☐

Persuade!

Create an advertisement to promote immigration to the UK.

Value 1 point ☐

Name: _____   Date: _____

Focus: _____

Create and choose a selection of tasks to the value of six points.

Organise!	**Investigate!**	**Compose!**	**Articulate!**
Value ☐ points	Value ☐ points	Value ☐ points	Value ☐ points
Perform!	**Create!**	**Write!**	**Persuade!**
Value ☐ points	Value ☐ points	Value ☐ points	Value ☐ points

Focus: How are plants and animals the same? How are they different?

Choose one activity from each section to show what you know about:
- the similarities and differences among plants and animals
- the features of plants and animals that are necessary for survival
- the impact of people on endangered species.

Write and draw

(graphic organiser) (labelled diagram) (Kidspiration/Kidspix)

(drawing or painting) (personal pledge) (letter) (report)

I chose _____

because _____

Preparation_____

Make and do

(mobile) (diorama) (role-play)

(board game) (3D dice) (puppet show)

I chose _____

because _____

Preparation _____

Say or sing

(interview) (talkback radio show)

(jingle, rap or song) (speech)

I chose _____

because _____

Preparation _____

Name:	Date:

Focus: _____

Create and choose activities for each section to show what you know about:

- _____

- _____

- _____

Write and draw

graphic organiser   labelled diagram   Kidspiration/Kidspix
drawing or painting   personal pledge   letter   report

I chose _____

because _____

Preparation _____

Make and do

mobile   diorama   role-play
board game   3D dice   puppet show

I chose _____

because _____

Preparation _____

Say or sing

interview   talkback radio show
jingle, rap or song   speech

I chose _____

because _____

Preparation _____

Name:	Date:

Focus: How do we measure weather?

- Choose three tasks, one from each group: see, hear and do.

- Show how well you worked by drawing a face in the circle.

Design a travel advertisement about a place with a very cold or very hot climate for magazine or radio. Consider using the computer.

See

Create a soundscape using instruments or objects to show different sorts of weather.

Hear

Make chart showing the weather over a week.

Do

Create symbols for different types of weather.

See

Tape record a weather report and write your own, predicting the weather.

Hear

Make a simple flag or wind sock that will show which way the wind is blowing.

Do

Name: _____ Date: _____

Focus: _____

- Write tasks for each group. Choose one task from each group.

- Show how well you worked by drawing a face in the circle.

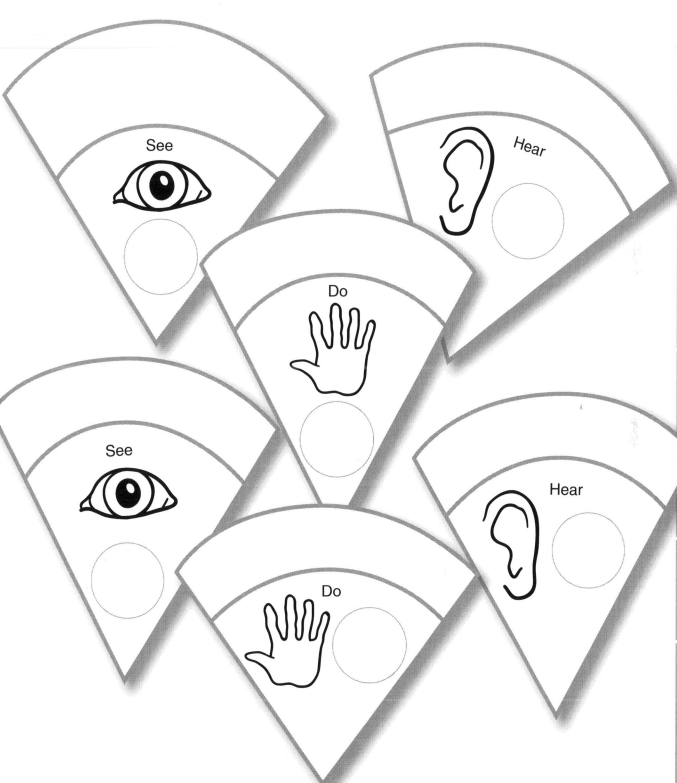

27

Focus: How can I help someone?

Think about someone who you can help: a family member, a friend, someone in your neighbourhood or someone you don't even know.

THINK about it

I am thinking about:_____

DO something about it

What could you do that might help this person? Be realistic and decide on something that is achievable.

What will you do?_____

When will you do it?_____

How will you do it?_____

What will you need?_____

Will anyone else need to be involved or informed?_____

_____

HOW do you FEEL about it?

How did you feel when you helped someone? Draw or write about your feelings.

How do you think the person you helped felt? _____

How do you know?_____

Learning preferences

Think, do, feel

Name: _____   Date: _____

Focus: _____

THINK about it

I am thinking about:_____

_____

_____

What will you do?_____

_____

DO something about it

When will you do it?_____

_____

How will you do it?_____

_____

What will you need?_____

_____

Will anyone else need to be involved or informed?_____

_____

_____

_____

HOW do you FEEL about it?

How do you feel about it now?_____

_____

How might others feel about it?_____

_____

Focus: How do we entertain ourselves?

Choose one activity from the box that best suits your style of learning.

Concrete sequential

* Make a **PowerPoint presentation** summarising different entertainment activities. ☐
* Create a **timetable** for a week showing your idea of a good balance between work and entertainment activities for someone your age. ☐
* Design a **flow chart** or diagram showing the consequences of being involved in an entertainment activity, for example, going to the movies or a football game. Be ready to discuss with someone else. ☐

Concrete random

* Make a **cube**. On each face write a question you could ask people about hobbies. In a small group, take turns to roll the cube and answer the questions. ☐
* Create a **collage** of people involved in different entertainment professions. ☐
* Design a **brochure** showing different kinds of entertainment opportunities in your community. ☐
* **Collect** examples of advertisements for various forms of entertainment from newspapers and magazines. ☐

Abstract sequential

* Write a **proposal** to the council requesting more entertainment facilities in your community. ☐
* Design a **slogan** that summarises why people should make time in their lives for entertainment. ☐
* Create a **picture** that represents 'entertainment' in the future. What might be done differently? ☐

Abstract random

* Devise a **performance** that could entertain others. ☐
* Conduct **interviews** with different age groups about their entertainment preferences. What are the most popular forms for different age groups? ☐
* Choose a **metaphor** or object that represents your understandings about entertainment. ☐

Why did you choose the activity?_____

_____

_____

Learning preferences

What's your style?

Name: _____ Date: _____

Focus: _____

Number the boxes 1 – 4 to show the kinds of activities you like to do (most to least). Then choose one activity to do from the box that best suits your style of learning.

Concrete sequential ☐

* ★ Make a PowerPoint presentation ☐
* ★ Outline ideas ☐
* ★ Design a flow chart or other diagram ☐

Concrete random ☐

* ★ Make up questions ☐
* ★ Make a collage ☐
* ★ Design a card ☐

Abstract sequential ☐

* ★ Write a proposal ☐
* ★ Design a slogan ☐
* ★ Create images ☐

Abstract random ☐

* ★ Act out an idea ☐
* ★ Conduct an interview ☐
* ★ Write metaphors ☐

Why did you choose the activity? _____

_____

_____

_____

_____

_____

Learning preferences

The artist's choice

Focus: What are wetlands? Why are they important?

Select one way that you would like to show what you know about wetlands.

Musician
Select music that you think 'sounds like' a wetlands area. Or create your own soundscape or piece of music to represent wetlands.

Painter
Paint a painting of wetlands and the animal and plant life found there.

Photographer
Visit a wetlands area and take some photos. Create a slideshow or collage using your photos.

Dancer
Create a dance piece, or a series of movements, that represents wetlands life.

Animator
Using a computer program, create an animation to show what you know about a wetlands plant or animal.

Sculptor
Create a 3D model to show life in and around wetlands.

Cartoonist
Create a cartoon sequence to show a 'day in the life' of wetlands or the animals that live there.

I have chosen to be a _____

because _____

I want my artwork to communicate the following important ideas:

_____

I will need the following equipment or resources to complete my artwork:

_____

Name:	Date:

Focus: _____

Think of a way that you would like to show what you know about your focus question.

Musician

Painter

Photographer

Dancer

Animator

Sculptor

Cartoonist

I have chosen to be a _____

because _____

I want my artwork to communicate the following important ideas:

_____

I will need the following equipment or resources to complete my artwork:

_____

Think about it! – Independent learning tasks

Task	Focus question/Area	Brief description	Year level
Bloom's activity choices page 40	*What makes a good structure?* Science & technology	Students choose three activities that involve remembering, understanding, analysing, creating, evaluating and/or applying.	Middle
The six thinking hats page 42	*How does advertising affect us?* Health & wellbeing	Students choose from a range of activities using the different coloured hats and creative, critical and reflective thinking.	Middle / Upper
The coloured thinking hats page 44	*What is a safe risk?* Health & wellbeing	Students use the coloured hats to structure thinking. A question to prompt each sort of thinking is given.	Lower
Thinking in different ways page 46	*How did Charlotte's Web make me think?* Society & environment	Students are prompted to be curious, precise, adventurous, organised and metacognitive when reflecting on the text.	Upper
The thinking gears page 48	*How do I learn?* Health & wellbeing	Students use thinking dispositions and choose more than one 'gear' to structure their thinking about learning.	Upper
Using the thinker's keys page 50	*What is an inventor?* Science & technology	Students choose three activities and ways to present their work developing creative, reflective and critical thinking.	Middle / Upper
The thinker's keys page 52	*What can we change?* Science & technology	Students choose three thinker's keys activities and utilise different thinking skills: creative, reflective and/or critical.	Lower
Tic tac toe page 54	*How do I make decisions?* Health & wellbeing	Students choose three activities from among the nine thinking skills: classifying, designing, hypothesising, imagining, reflecting, questioning, critiquing, evaluating and synthesising.	Middle / Upper
Mix and match page 56	*What do I think about thinking?* Health & wellbeing	Students choose among twelve activities relating to four different types of thinking.	Middle / Upper
Thinking over it page 58	*What did I learn this term?* Health & wellbeing	Students choose from among three categories: creative, reflective and critical thinking. They respond to question prompts to help improve their writing.	Middle / Upper
Thinking graphically page 60	*How can we live more sustainably?* Society & environment	Students choose graphic organisers to help them think about and represent their understandings.	Middle / Upper

Support materials for independent learning tasks with a focus on thinking: 1 Keeping track of tasks; 3 Record of conversations with and observations of students; 4 My weekly diary; 5 My individual record sheet; 6 Free choice tickets and free choice tickets record sheet; 7 Creating independent learning tasks; 8 Ideas for developing independent learning activities; 9 Ideas for resourcing play-based learning activities; 10 Using modes: activity menus; 12 My contract; 18 Independent learner prompt cards; 19 Trouble shooting poster and cards; 20 Reminders for group work; 21 What kind of learner have I been today?; 22 Managing your time checklist; 23 My learning journal; 24 My double entry journal; 26 Learning review lucky dip cards.

Think about it!
A focus on thinking

Theorists categorise or organise thinking skills in different ways. The various frameworks presented here use a range of thinking taxonomies, theories, skills and strategies. A wide range of independent learning tasks is included so that students can explore and become aware of different thinking skills. Some learning tasks are clearly designed to cater for a particular framework. Others are a mixture of frameworks or present new strategies for students to try. The tasks also offer strategies to develop students' thinking and assist students to learn about different ways to organise their ideas.

We have chosen three broad headings to categorise thinking skills:

- reflective thinking and metacognition
- creative thinking
- logical and critical thinking.

The table that follows has been developed to assist teachers with planning links among the thinking types, the associated skills and possible activities. These lists are not exhaustive, nor do they indicate that types of thinking should be discrete. Thinking usually involves skills in more than one category. In addition, skills such as synthesising could involve creative or critical thinking. Similarly, strategies can be used for multiple purposes. However, in order to avoid repetition, the skills and strategies have been listed in one category only.

Reflective thinking and metacognition				
Self-questioning	Questioning	Action plans	Making decisions	
Applying ideas to another situation	Recalling	Summarising		
Reviewing and revising	Thinking about others' feelings and perspectives			
Thinking ethically	Thinking empathically			
Possible activities				
De Bono's shoes and hats	Debate	Question dice	Brainstorm (list, describe, name)	
Role-play	Conscience game			
Useful graphic organisers				
Concept map	Cluster web	Spider diagram	Bridge	Comic strip CTG graph

Creative thinking				
Creating original ideas	Adapting ideas: adding, expanding, changing			
Finding and considering alternatives and solutions	Challenging assumptions			
Imagining	Predicting	Hypothesising		
Planning	Inventing			
Possible activities				
Forced relationship/ridiculous association	BAR key (Bigger, Add, Remove)			
Reverse key	Visualise			
SCAMPER (Substitute, Combine, Adapt, Modify, Magnify, Minify, Put another way, Eliminate, Reverse)				

Logical and critical thinking				
Organising	Classifying	Analysing	Examining	Critiquing
Generalising	Hypothesising	Synthesising	Evaluating/ judging	Sequencing
Ranking	Prioritising	Establishing cause and effect	Inferring	Interpreting
Possible activities				
Considering different viewpoints	Reasoning	Bundling		
Fat and skinny questions	Metaphors	Story map		
Useful graphic organisers				
Cluster web	T-chart	Y-chart	Venn diagram	Balancing scales
Data chart	Ranking	PMI	SWOT	Cycle circle	Twister
Flow chart	Continuum	Consequence or futures wheel		

Thinking dispositions

Thinking dispositions can be described as the tendency or pattern of cognitive actions expressed by behaviour. These are context specific and not personality traits, for example the tendency to approach thinking with precision or open-mindedness. These tendencies are displayed frequently over time. Effective thinkers tend to be curious, critical, explorative, inquiring and to question, reason, clarify, organise and reflect on ideas and their own thinking. They are open-minded and creative in their thinking.

The following table synthesises some of the commonly identified dispositions. The questions in the table describe how a person with this disposition might typically use questioning and self-questioning when approaching an issue or problem.

Be curious	What do I wonder about? What problems or issues are raised? What questions should I ask the author/producer/designer/artist/inventor?
Be precise	What am I sure about? What examples can I give to explain or justify my thoughts? Are there any gaps in what I know? What could I explain to others about this? What are the facts?
Be open-minded	What are some different perspectives? What is something I have never thought of before? What was unexpected or surprising? What would I say/do differently?
Be organised	How can I sequence ideas or issues from start to end? What do I need to do to find out more? What do I need to do next? How could I solve this problem?
Be reflective and metacognitive	How will I sum up my ideas? How have my thinking and feelings changed? Have I answered my questions or do I have new questions? What do I know that I didn't know before? How effective was my thinking? What has influenced my thinking? What kind of thinking might I need to do more of? What do I believe?
Be empathic	How do others feel about this? What are some other points of view? Is there a way of seeing this differently? How might this affect others? Are my views shared? By whom?

Thinking gears

The thinking gears were developed by the cognitive skills group at Harvard University's 'Project Zero'. The gears act as metaphors for thinking dispositions. They provide a fun and alternative way to describe the different attitudes or ways of approaching a problem. The gears represent ways to 'move' through a problem or challenge. The gears are often used to encourage students to self-assess – to think about how they are working through or how they have worked through a particular task.

Adventure gear	Are you trying something new? Are you thinking of new possibilities and alternatives?
Detective gear	Are you asking yourself questions and analysing the information?
Explanation gear	Are you making links? Are you comparing and contrasting and looking for cause and effect?
Strategy gear	Are you planning ahead? Are you organising your thinking and doing and making plans?
Timing gear	Are you looking at the big picture and asking what will happen if ...? Are you thinking about where and when all this might end?
Proving gear	Are you gathering evidence? Can you provide examples and illustrations?
Metacognitive gear	Are you thinking about the kind of thinking you are doing? Are you noticing the way you are going about things and changing thinking if necessary?

Bloom's taxonomy

Bloom's taxonomy of cognitive processes, which was created in the 1950s to encourage higher order thinking, has been revised. In the following table, the original and revised versions are noted.

Original version	Revised version	Processes	Verb stems
Knowledge	**Remembering**	Recalling factual information	name, state, define, repeat, list, recall
Comprehension	**Understanding**	Understanding information	explain, identify, describe, compare, report, outline, tell, locate, review
Application	**Applying**	Using previously learned knowledge, concepts, principles or theories in new situations	apply, practise, use, demonstrate, illustrate, dramatise, interpret
Analysis	**Analysing**	Breaking information into parts and showing an understanding among the parts	analyse, contrast, compare, question, debate, relate, examine, identify
Evaluation	**Evaluating**	Generating new ideas, planning and producing	compose, propose, suggest, plan, design, construct, invent, formulate, create, arrange, prepare
Synthesis	**Creating**	Critiquing, making a judgement	judge, assess, decide, rate, evaluate, measure, estimate, choose

De Bono's thinking hats

De Bono's six coloured hats thinking structure is well known for systematically encouraging different types of thinking.

Hats	Description	Example questions
White hat	Information, facts, figures, questions	What facts have you learnt? What information do you need?
Yellow hat	Good points, positives	What did you do really well?
Black hat	Bad points, negatives, caution, judgements	What things could you have done better? What do you need to be careful about?
Red hat	Emotions, feelings, intuition	How do you feel about your work?
Green hat	Creativity, new ideas, suggestions, proposals	What could you have done differently? What are some ways to work it out?
Blue hat	Thinking about and organising thinking	What sort of thinking would be useful now?

Thinker's keys

Tony Ryan designed the thinker's keys to motivate students to use a range of thinking types, particularly creative thinking. The keys can be used to design questions and independent thinking activities.

Reverse key: things you would never/cannot see or find in the situation under discussion	**Alphabet key:** relevant words starting with all the letters of the alphabet
BAR key: Bigger; Add; Remove, Reduce or Replace to improve the design of everyday objects	**What if? key:** posing questions – literal, ridiculous or creative
Brainstorming key: a list of solutions to a stated problem	**Commonalities key:** the commonalities between any two objects
Forced relationship key: considering the attributes of dissimilar objects to develop a solution to a problem	**Interpretation key:** unusual situations and different explanations for the situation
Brick wall key: statements accepted as true, unquestioned and undisputed are stated and then challenged	**Variations key:** searching for many ways to solve a problem
Combination key: the attributes of two dissimilar objects are combined to develop a new or better product	**Question key:** pose an answer first and then list questions to match
Inventions key: develop an invention with unusual materials and/or in an unusual way	**Alternatives key:** ways that a task can be completed without using the usual tools
Picture key: using a picture or diagram to try to work out any ways that it might be connected to the topic	**Ridiculous key:** making a ridiculous statement and then trying to substantiate it
Disadvantages key: listing disadvantages and then trying to reduce disadvantages or find connections between them	**Prediction key:** thinking about the range of possible outcomes of a situation
Construction key: considering the creative use of some everyday materials	**Different uses key:** being creative about different possible uses of objects

Thinking

Bloom's activity choices

Focus: What makes a good structure?

Complete at least three activities. They should be from different boxes.

Remembering

* On a world map, mark the location of 10 famous, human-made structures. ☐

* Choose a structure you know (your house, your school, etc). Write a list of all the materials used in the structure. ☐

Understanding

* Choose one famous structure. Why was it built? ☐

* Name some structures that do not serve the purpose for which they were originally designed. What are they used for now? ☐

Analysing

* What are some of the things that need to be taken into account when designing a structure that will be in a public space? ☐

* Imagine you are building a new school. What advice do you need? Who would you ask for advice? ☐

Creating

* You are an architect given the responsibility of creating a new structure (such as the athletes' village for the next Olympic Games). What would it look like? Write a letter to the board to explain your idea. ☐

* Complete an action plan for relocating the school to put up a new hospital. ☐

Evaluating

* Make a list of criteria to evaluate two famous structures. ☐

* Choose a structure that is controversial. Make a list of positives and negatives from different people's perspectives. ☐

Applying

* Design a new structure for part of your school that will be visually appealing and serve a useful purpose. ☐

* If you were to rebuild a famous city structure, what would it be and how and why would you change it? ☐

Name: _____   Date: _____

Focus: _____

Write at least three activities. They should be in different boxes.

Remembering	**Understanding**
★ List _____ ★ Name _____ _____	★ Describe _____ ★ Explain _____ _____
Analysing	**Creating**
★ Compare _____ ★ Examine _____ _____	★ Invent _____ ★ Design _____ _____
Evaluating	**Applying**
★ Rate _____ ★ Assess _____ _____	★ Use _____ ★ Demonstrate _____ _____

Focus: How does advertising affect us?

Choose question/s from each hat. See your teacher to negotiate how many questions you will do.

White hat: the facts

How many advertisements are there per hour on a commercial TV channel? ☐

How long do advertisements go for? ☐

What is advertised during children's programs after school? ☐

What are the regulations governing advertising to children? ☐

Red hat: the feelings

How do some advertisements make us feel? Why? What techniques do advertisers use to make people feel a certain way? Give an example. ☐

How do you feel about the advertising of junk food on television? Why? ☐

Yellow hat: the benefits

What are the benefits of advertising? ☐

Find examples of advertisements that make a positive difference to people's lives. ☐

Why are advertisements good for us? Argue the case. ☐

Black hat: the problems

What are some of the problems that advertising creates? ☐

How do advertisements negatively affect children? ☐

Green hat: the solutions

How could we address some of the problems that advertisements create? ☐

How can we help people become more aware of the need to think carefully when they read or view advertisements? ☐

What could you do to lessen the influence of advertisements on you? ☐

Blue hat: the thinking

How can you use the six hats to help you think about an advertisement you are watching? ☐

What hat do you 'wear' when you watch advertisements? ☐

What has this got you thinking more about? ☐

Name:	Date:

Focus: _____

Write a question for each hat about your focus question.

White hat: the facts

_____
_____
_____

Red hat: the feelings

_____
_____
_____

Yellow hat: the benefits

_____
_____
_____

Black hat: the problems

_____
_____
_____

Green hat: the solutions

_____
_____
_____

Blue hat: the thinking

_____
_____
_____

Thinking

The coloured thinking hats

Focus: What is a safe risk?

Use the coloured hats to think about taking risks.

White hat:
the facts

List or draw some safe and unsafe risks that you have taken.

Red hat:
the feelings

Think about a risk that was successful. How did you feel before and after taking the risk?

Black hat:
the problems

What are some safe risks you could take with your learning?

Green hat:
the solutions

What are some of the possible problems when taking risks?

Name: _____ Date: _____

Focus: _____

Write a question for each hat about your focus question.

Focus: How did *Charlotte's Web* make me think?

Read the book by EB White. Use the prompts from each of the ways of thinking to help you reflect on the text. Discuss and record your responses.

Thinking

Thinking in different ways

| **Be curious** |
| What issues are raised in the book? For example, loyalty, friendship, honesty. |
| Think about a place in the text that made you wonder about the behaviour of |
| an individual. For example, why did Templeton act the way he did? |
| What questions would you ask Charlotte and other characters? |

| **Be precise** |
| Think about something that you would do to help a friend. |
| Try to give an example from your own life. |
| What do you need to think more about to be able to explain events/actions? |

| **Be adventurous** |
| What are some different ways of looking at the way |
| the people and animals treated each other? |
| What is something you would have done differently if |
| you were a character or the author? |

| **Be organised** |
| What do you believe was the most important event/phrase in the book? |
| How do you feel about what happens at the end of the story? |
| What part do you need to revisit to clarify your ideas? |

| **Be metacognitive** |
| How would you sum up your ideas about friendship? |
| How have your thinking and feelings about a character changed? |
| What do you know that you didn't know before? |
| What questions do you now have? |
| How effective was your thinking and ways of organising your |
| own thinking about issues in the text? |

© J Wilson & K Murdoch 2009 **Learning for Themselves** Routledge

Name: _____   Date: _____

Focus: _____

Think about a book you have read. Choose some prompts from each of the ways of thinking to help you pose questions and reflect on the text.

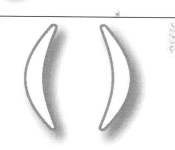

Be curious
What do I wonder about?
What problems/issues are raised?
What questions would I ask the author?
Be precise
What am I sure about?
What examples can I give to explain/justify my thoughts?
Are there any gaps in what I know? (reread the text to check)
Be adventurous
What are some different perspectives?
What is something I have never thought of before?
Be organised
How can I sequence my ideas/issues from start to end?
What do I believe?
How do I feel?
What do I need to do to find out more?
Be metacognitive
How would I sum up the author's ideas?
How have my thinking and feelings changed?
Have I answered my questions? Do I have new questions?
What do I know that I didn't know before?
How effective was my thinking?

Name: Date:

Focus: How do I learn?

Choose one gear to help you reflect on your own learning. Then change gears and think about your learning in a different way. Try them all if you can.

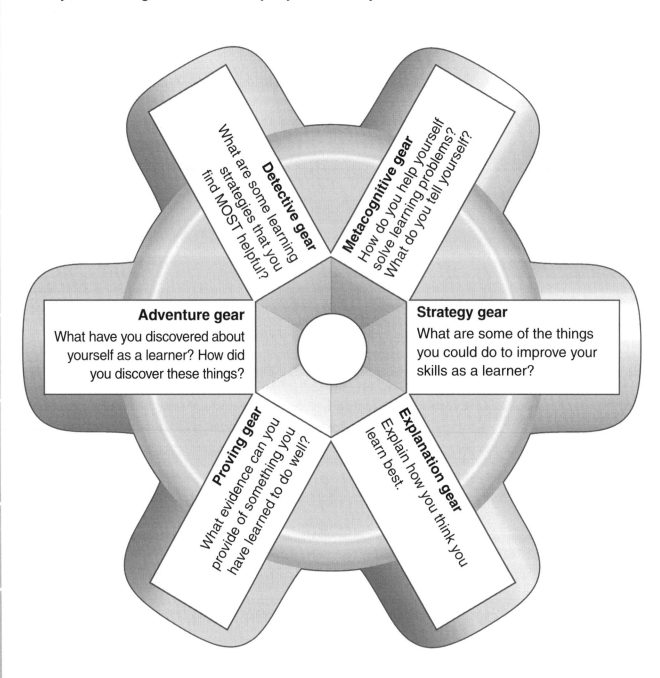

Detective gear
What are some learning strategies that you find MOST helpful?

Metacognitive gear
How do you help yourself solve learning problems? What do you tell yourself?

Adventure gear
What have you discovered about yourself as a learner? How did you discover these things?

Strategy gear
What are some of the things you could do to improve your skills as a learner?

Proving gear
What evidence can you provide of something you have learned to do well?

Explanation gear
Explain how you think you learn best.

Name: _____   Date: _____

Focus: _____

Choose one gear to help you reflect. Then change gears and think in a different way.
Try them all if you can.

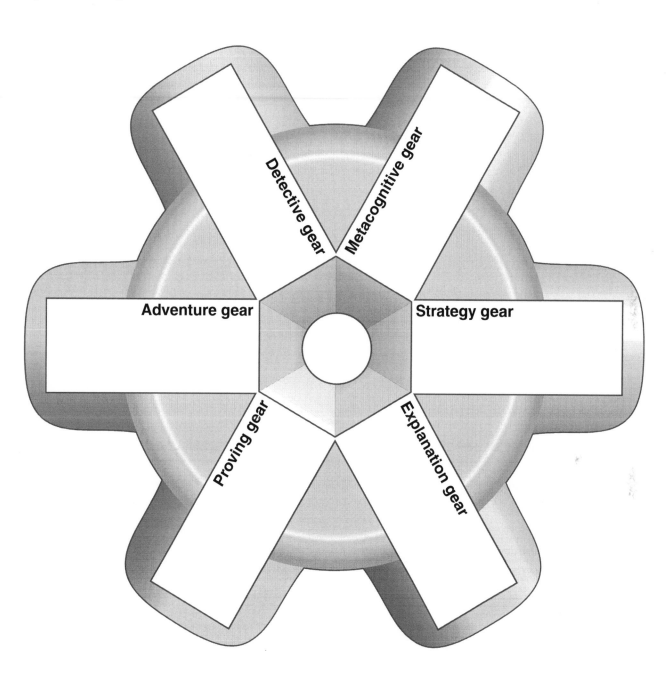

Name: Date:

Focus: What is an inventor?

Choose three thinker's key activities. Then choose a way to present your work.

Thinker's keys

Presentation options

Reverse key

What are 10 things you think an
inventor would never do?

role-play
rap
song
poem
true/false statements

What if? key

What if you were an inventor.
What would you invent and why?

poster
letter
reflective journal entry
newspaper article
interview

Question key

The answer is inventor.
What are the questions?

listing questions
survey people's ideas
poem

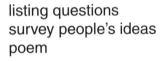

BAR key

Choose any product. Make a part
Bigger, Add a part and Remove a part.
What have you invented?

cartoon
labelled diagram
graphic organisers

Inventions key

Think of something that has never
been invented. Think about using
unusual materials.

labelled diagram
make a model
draw or paint

Commonalities key

What are the commonalities
between a toothbrush and a car?

Venn diagram
scales
graphic organiser
data chart

Alternatives key

In what ways could you invent
something without using the
usual tools?

multiple choice quiz questions
flow chart
cause and effect map

| Name: | Date: |

Focus: _____

Think of three different thinker's key activities. Then choose a way to present your work.

| **Thinker's keys** | **Presentation options** |

Reverse key

What are 10 things you should never

do when _____

role-play
rap
song
poem
true/false statements

What if? key

Be creative. What are your questions
and a range of answers?

poster
letter
reflective journal entry
newspaper article
interview

Question key

The answer is _____.
What are the questions?

listing questions
survey people for their ideas
poem

Picture key

Choose a picture/s or draw an image
related to your topic.

cartoon
collage
paper mosaic
graphic organisers

Inventions key

Using different types of products, invent
something related to your topic.

labelled diagram
make a model
draw or paint

Commonalities key

What are the commonalities between

_____ and _____?

Venn diagram
scales
graphic organiser
data chart

Alternatives key

Brainstorm some different ways to

_____.

multiple choice quiz questions
flow chart
cause and effect map

Focus: What can we change?

Choose three different thinker's key activities. Draw or write your answers.

Alphabet key

Make a list of foods beginning with each letter of the alphabet. Mark the ones that have reversible change.

BAR key (Bigger, Add, Remove)

Change a recipe: make a part Bigger, Add something and Remove an ingredient.
What's the result?

What if? key

What if all changes in cooking were reversible? How would this change your life?

Brainstorming key

What things would you like to change about the foods we eat?

Question key

The answer is change.
What is the question?

Different uses key

What are 10 different ways to change an egg?

Inventions key

Invent an experiment that could show how ice or another substance can change from a solid to a liquid and a gas.

Commonalities key

Choose two household substances. What do they have in common?

Thinking

The thinker's keys

Name: _____ Date: _____

Focus: _____

Write three different thinker's key activities. Draw or write your answers.

Alphabet key

BAR key (Bigger, Add, Remove)

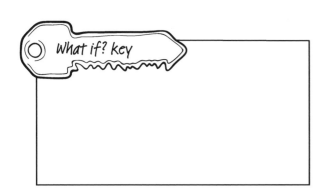

What if? key

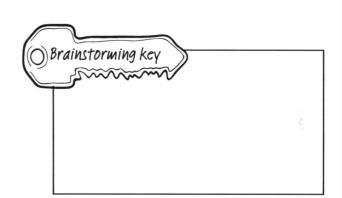

Brainstorming key

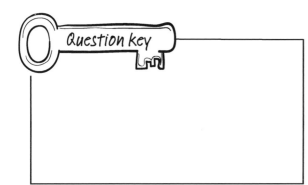

Question key

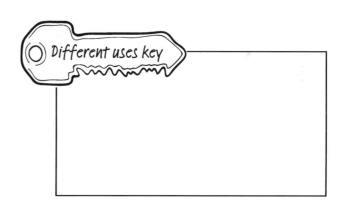

Different uses key

Inventions key

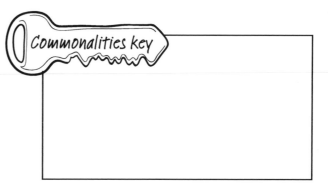

Commonalities key

Thinking

The thinker's keys

Focus: How do I make decisions?

Choose three activities in a row to complete.

Design  Design a flow chart for making decisions. List step by step.	**Classify**  Brainstorm all the decisions you might make in one day. Classify them into groups using a data chart or cluster diagram.	**Hypothesise**  List three decisions you think will be difficult to make when you are older. Place them on a ladder in order of difficulty. Discuss with others.
Imagine  You are a famous historic figure. Think of a choice they made that has affected others. Imagine you had made a different choice. Use two cause and effect wheels to show the consequences of each.	**Reflect**  What decision have you made that you regret or wish you had made differently? Create a cartoon strip about what happened and what might have happened if you had done something differently.	**Question**  Think of a decision made at home, school, by yourself or others that you do not always agree with. Write a list of questions to find out why the decision was made.
Critique  Use the newspaper to find an article about a decision made by the government. Who was involved? What perspectives were considered? Who was not included? Who was affected? Rewrite the article.	**Evaluate**  Choose a decision made by you or that affects you. Use the scales graphic organiser to show the advantages and disadvantages.	**Synthesise**  Write a slogan that sums up the effect of a decision or draw an image with you in it.

Thinking

Tic tac toe

Name: _____   Date: _____

Focus: _____

Write three activities in a row to complete.

Design	Classify	Hypothesise
Imagine	**Reflect**	**Question**
Critique	**Evaluate**	**Synthesise**

Thinking

Tic tac toe

Name: Date:

Focus: What do I think about thinking?

Choose activities from each of the boxes to show what you know about thinking. Suggestions have been provided for representing your ideas.

The six coloured hats

Black and yellow: What sort of thinking do you do really well and not so well?

Suggestion: Make a T-chart.

White and red: What do you know about your own thinking? What sort of effort is required? What would be hard to do but you would like to try?

Suggestion: Create a very tiny book.

Blue and green: Rate your thinking capacity. If you could improve your thinking, who would you get to help you? Choose someone from history.

Suggestion: Conduct a mock interview with this person about how they might help you.

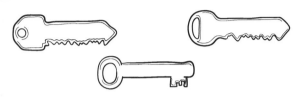

The thinker's keys

What if? key: What if humans had brains that worked twice as fast? What might they do with this thinking power?

Suggestion: Draw a labelled diagram.

Reverse key: What would a deep thinker never do?

Suggestion: Write a magazine article.

Disadvantages key: What are the disadvantages of being a methodical thinker?

Suggestion: Draw a cause and effect wheel.

Thinking gears

Adventure gear: List three things you have discovered about thinking.

Suggestion: Make up a rap.

Metacognitive gear: What have you noticed about your thinking?

Suggestion: Make a story map.

Proving gear: What evidence can you provide about your thinking development?

Suggestion: Make a list of criteria and attach it to a work sample.

Bloom's activity choices

Understanding: Explain why thinking skills are useful.

Suggestion: Write a poem.

Evaluate your improvement in thinking.
Suggestion: Give yourself a rating.

Creating: What advice would you give next year's students about thinking through tricky problems?

Suggestion: Write a manual.

Name: _____ Date: _____

Focus: _____

Show what you know about thinking. Write your own activities or do the suggestions provided for representing your ideas.

The six coloured hats

Black and yellow (problems and benefits)
Suggestion: Make a T-chart.

White and red (facts and feelings)
Suggestion: Create a very tiny book.

Blue and green (thinking and solutions)
Suggestion: Conduct a mock interview.

The thinker's keys

What if? key
Suggestion: Draw a labelled diagram.

Reverse key
Suggestion: Write a magazine article.

Disadvantages key
Suggestion: Draw a cause and effect wheel.

The thinking gears

Adventure gear
Suggestion: Make up a rap.

Metacognitive gear
Suggestion: Make a story map.

Proving gear
Suggestion: Make a list of criteria and attach it to a work sample.

Bloom's activity choices

Understanding
Suggestion: Write a poem.

Evaluate
Suggestion: Give yourself a rating.

Creating
Suggestion: Write a manual.

Mix and match

Focus: What did I learn this term?

Read all the questions and suggestions below before you start. Circle at least one from each column (critical, creative and reflective thinking) to help you write a review of the way you have worked this term.

Critical thinking	Creative thinking	Reflective thinking
Analyse the factors that assisted your learning this term. What were the most and least useful?	How could you change an aspect of your work to improve it?	What were your achievements?
What would be included on your summary of highlights and lowlights for this term?	What award would you get for your efforts this term?	What did you learn about or to do?
Compare two different lessons. What did you do that made a difference?	What is one part of your behaviour that you'd like to minify or magnify?	How would you rate your performance?
Evaluate your overall performance from someone else's viewpoint and your own. How well did you do?	If you could add a skill to help you learn, what would it be?	What do you want to find out more about?
Create a list of your attributes. Which one is the most important?	Draw you at work. What resources would help you get the job done better?	How/when will you use something you have learnt again?
If you continue to work the way you have been, what do you think the results might be?	Think of many ways to learn differently. Which ones could you try?	What did someone do or say that made you really think? Why?

Thinking

Thinking over it

Name: _____   Date: _____

Focus: _____

Read all the questions and suggestions below before you start. Circle at least one from each column (critical, creative and reflective thinking) to help you.

Critical thinking	Creative thinking	Reflective thinking
Analyse the factors that were the most and least useful.	How could you change one aspect to improve it?	What were your achievements?
What else could have been included?	What award would you get for your efforts?	What did you learn about or to do?
Compare two pieces of your work. How do they compare?	What is one part that you'd like to minify or magnify?	How would you rate your performance?
Overall, how would you evaluate it?	If you could add a skill to help you do this better, what would it be?	What do you want to find out more about or to do better?
Create a list. Which points are the most important?	What resources would help you get the job done better?	How/when will you use this again?
What feedback do you think you might get? What might the results be?	Think of ways to do things differently. Which ones could you try?	What did someone do or say that made you really think? Why?

Name: Date:

Focus: How can we live more sustainably?

Graphic organisers help us organise and show our thinking. Use them to plan, to solve a problem, to help answer a question or to think through something.

Try all the diagrams.

Choose one option from each to focus your thinking.

Spider diagram

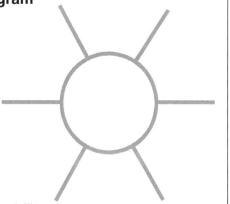

Brainstorm:
- Sustainability
- Environment
- Conservation

Consequence wheel

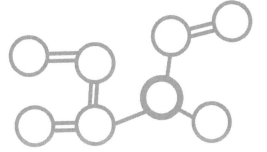

Explore the possible consequences of:
- having shorter showers
- refusing plastic bags
- riding a bike instead of driving
- planting an indigenous garden.

Flow chart

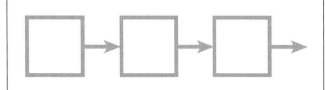

What steps could you take to:
- reduce the amount of paper used at school
- save water at home
- encourage people to car pool
- have a rubbish-free lunch policy at school.

Push and pull diagram

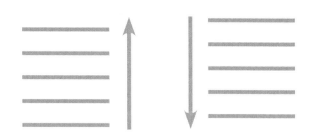

Choose a question.
- What are the things that help us make a positive difference to the environment?
- What are the things that make it difficult to live sustainably?

This is what I noticed about my thinking while I used the graphic organisers:

_____

_____

Focus: _____

Graphic organisers help us organise and show our thinking. Use them to plan, to solve a problem, to help answer a question or to think through something.

Use the diagrams to focus your thinking.

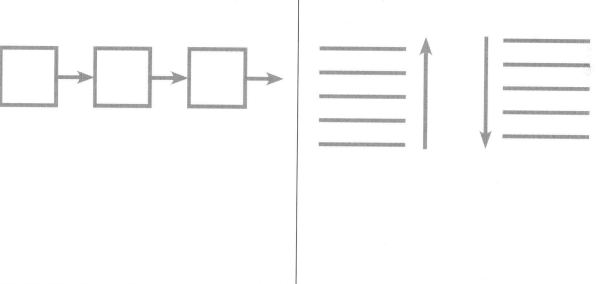

Spider diagram Brainstorm	**Consequence wheel** Explore the consequences
Flow chart Choose an action	**Push and pull diagram** Choose a question

This is what I noticed about my thinking while I used the graphic organisers:

_____

_____

I wonder … – Independent learning tasks

Task	Focus question/Area	Brief description	Year
Data chart page 66	*What can I learn about **spiders**?* Science & technology	Students record key information as they use several different texts. Then they make conclusions about what they have learned about the topic.	Lower
Question matrix page 68	*How can we create a **healthy community**?* Health & wellbeing	Students select key questions designed to help them investigate different aspects of a topic and pursue independent inquiry.	Upper
Resource detective page 70	*What makes your **community special**?* Society & environment	Students select various resources to help them learn more about a topic. They then select three that will be the most useful for an investigation.	Middle / Upper
Now I understand page 72	*How has **the UK changed**?* Society & environment	Students use a menu of activities to select a means by which they will show what they understand about a topic. Teachers provide the understanding goals and assessment criteria to guide student choices.	Upper
Voices of the people page 74	*What does it mean to take on a **challenge**?* Society & environment	This framework focuses on the skill of interviewing as a method of research. Students use both set and self-devised questions to interview various people about a topic and then draw some conclusions and reflect on their findings.	Middle / Upper
Must do, can do page 76	*How do **animals** survive in their environment?* Science & technology	This framework provides young students with a simple structure for planning their own inquiry into a question or topic of their choice. They design some questions, select ways to find out and choose from a simple menu, their method of communicating what they have learned.	Lower
My passion project page 78		This framework provides several prompts and guidelines to support students who are planning an investigation into a topic of their choosing.	Middle / Upper

Support materials for independent learning tasks with a focus on inquiry: 2 Record of teacher/student conferences and stages completed; 3 Record of conversations with and observations of students; 4 My weekly diary; 5 My individual record sheet; 10 Using modes: activity menus; 11 My own investigation – questions to ask; 12 My contract; 14 Planning and reflecting; 16 Presentation planner and assessment sheet; 17 Teacher auditing checklist; 18 Independent learner prompt cards; 19 Trouble shooting poster and cards; 21 What kind of learner have I been today?; 22 Managing your time checklist; 23 My learning journal; 24 My double entry journal.

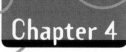

Chapter 4

I wonder ...
A focus on inquiry

The emphasis of the following independent learning tasks is on assisting students to gather, critique, analyse, synthesise and reflect on information they gain, often from several sources. In these tasks, the dominant role of the student is as *researcher* or *inquirer* and there is a strong focus on being able to access and make sense of information from various sources as well as on structuring and sequencing how an inquiry will proceed and be applied to life within and beyond school.

Inquiry-based approaches to curriculum design, teaching and learning have become increasingly popular in schools. Essentially, inquiry learning engages students in actively investigating questions of interest and significance. These questions may be posed by the student or developed in collaboration with teachers or fellow students. Inquiry learning is also characterised by the engagement of students in a broad sequence of phases rather than a host of 'activities'. While the labels used to describe the phases of inquiry vary, there is general agreement that the process is a sequential one that builds upon students' prior knowledge and often ends in some kind of real 'action' or application using the understandings and skills gained through the investigation.

By its very nature, an inquiry approach to teaching and learning both *fosters* and *requires* independence in student learning. As they work through the process, students must navigate their way through the challenges of accessing appropriate resources, sorting through the information they gain, synthesising, reflecting and acting on their understandings. This approach, pioneered by significant educators such as Bruner (1966) and Dewey (1938), is recognised as a powerful method for curriculum planning and classroom practices. Importantly, the precursors of this approach recognised decades ago that teaching must be about developing students' capacity to think and learn independently and, ultimately, to be able to inquire for themselves.

> *To instruct someone ... is not a matter of getting him to commit results to mind. Rather, it is to teach him to participate in the process that makes possible the estab nowledge ... Knowing is a process not a product.*
> (Bruner 1966: 72)

Some fifty years on, teachers continue to use inquiry as a framework for planning units of work that explore questions. While an inquiry approach mirrors the natural process of learning that takes place within the human brain, the skills and strategies that formalise this process in school need to be carefully scaffolded and modelled by teachers. We encourage teachers to develop units of inquiry that demonstrate to students how they can take a question, hypothesis or proposition and then work through a process to gain deeper understanding. When students have been involved in shared inquiries, and when teachers are explicit in their modelling of how we can effectively inquire, students are more able to conduct their *own* inquiries using structures such as those presented in this chapter.

Phase of inquiry	Typical student actions
Identifying questions/ issues to be explored or establishing a hypothesis	Constructing questions; sharing ideas with others; hypothesising; listening; predicting; estimating; setting goals; expressing thoughts and feelings; reflecting on and describing prior experiences/knowledge; recalling information and experiences; theorising
Identifying resources and a plan of action that can be used to explore the questions – organising to 'find out'	Organising events or visits; communicating with a range of people in appropriate ways: writing letters, sending faxes, emails, phone calls, etc; identifying appropriate information sources; locating relevant information within a source; using information technology; planning; thinking ahead; managing time and resources; justifying; making choices
Gathering and recording information from resources	Observing/monitoring; questioning; summarising and note taking; comparing and contrasting; listening; reading; viewing; inferring; recognising bias; critically analysing texts; working collaboratively and independently; being systematic and organised; recording and storing information
Processing or sorting through information gathered	Organising and classifying ideas/information; seeing patterns; thinking laterally and creatively; representing ideas in a range of ways; working independently and collaboratively; presenting ideas to others; interpreting information; analysing; making choices; explaining; reporting; ordering events; testing and checking; identifying similarities and differences; recognising themes and patterns; recognising different points of view
Synthesising and concluding	Generalising; connecting key ideas; revising, reflecting and restating; providing feedback; summarising; justifying; elaborating; expressing thoughts and feelings; working cooperatively; making choices; representing ideas to others; interpreting ideas; persuading; designing
Reflecting and acting	Recalling; identifying feelings and emotions; identifying how ideas have changed over time; self-assessing; peer assessing; setting future goals; expressing feelings and understandings to others; linking new learning to local and global issues; identifying strengths and weaknesses; identifying and articulating what learning has taken place and how; decision-making; devising an action plan; planning ahead; working to a time line; considering options; responding to the work of others; framing new questions; evaluating materials and experiences

The table outlines the broad phases associated with inquiry and the skills commonly required by each phase. There is general agreement that inquiry-based learning does involve a broadly sequential process. However, it is also highly 'recursive' in that students will often move backwards and forwards among the phases as they travel towards deeper understanding. It is important that students themselves recognise the stages they are moving through. This language should be made explicit to students so they can better self-manage the process.

Not just 'units of work'

It is common practice in schools for the inquiry approach to be implemented through 'units of work' that explore generative and often interdisciplinary questions or issues. These units are generally implemented over a sustained period of time and can often form the 'backbone' of curriculum work in a class (especially in the primary setting).

It is important to recognise, however, that inquiry is not simply about 'units of work'. The sequence, skills and processes outlined in the table can be manifested in all sorts of arrangements for learning that may look and feel quite different to a unit of work. Many teachers of students in the early years, for example, foster inquiry through designing a play-based programme. They may use materials and experiences to provoke questioning and wondering. As students' interests are identified, tasks may be planned or provided to allow them to pursue a pathway of interest and the pathway may be 'travelled' for a short or extended period. In this kind of arrangement, students may be pursuing several smaller inquiries during a similar timeframe. The planning for these small inquiries may occur on a daily rather than weekly basis.

While it is often associated with an integrated approach to curriculum, inquiry can also take place within a single discipline or subject. This is an approach that is essentially about helping students learn *how* to learn and is a process that is transferable across a broad range of contexts.

Name: _____   Date: _____

Focus: What can I learn about spiders?

Research spiders using books, DVDs, websites or people. Record the information you find out.

	Spiders are ...	Spiders have ...	Spiders can ...	Spiders need ...	Types of spiders
What do I already think about this?					
Resource 1:					
Resource 2:					
Resource 3:					
Summary statement: What can I now say about this?					

Name:		Date:

Focus: _____

Research your topic using books, DVDs, websites or people. Record the information you find out.

Types of ____	____ **need …**	____ **can …**	____ **have …**	____ **are …**
What do I already think about this?				
Resource 1:				
Resource 2:				
Resource 3:				
Summary statement: What can I now say about this?				

© J Wilson & K Murdoch 2009 **Learning for Themselves** Routledge

Data chart

Inquiry

Question matrix

Focus: How can we create a healthy community?

Choose at least three activities from different rows and columns.

	Event	Situation	Choice	Person	Reason	Means
Present	What are the biggest health risks of people in your age group?	Where can you go to participate in sport in your community?	How can people help to make their communities healthy?	Who do you admire for their healthy lifestyle? Why?	Why is it important to consider people's emotional health?	How is it possible that there are still unhealthy people in our community?
Past	What are some old cures for illnesses? Why were they used?	Where did your parents participate in sport in their childhood?	What affected people's choice of food and drink 100 years ago?	Who were some of the significant people that made medical advances in health?	Why has medical science improved your prospects for good health?	How was your grandparents' childhood health different to yours?
Possibility	What could society do to encourage people to lead a healthy lifestyle?	Where could you find out information that could help you lead a healthy lifestyle?	Which organisation would you choose to help with a mental health issue? Why?	Who has an effect on our healthy lifestyle? How?	Why can it be difficult for people to maintain a healthy lifestyle?	How can you improve your own health?
Probability	If a child did not have a healthy diet, what would the long term effects be?	Where might you be able to purchase the most healthy food?	Which outside social pressures affect what you eat?	Who could advise you on a good diet?	Why do some people choose to take performance enhancing drugs?	How would your family be affected if they couldn't afford healthy food?
Prediction	What health issues might be important in 50 years time? What current issue may be irrelevant?	Where will the world's healthiest people live in the future?	Which food choice will you be unlikely to ever make?	What if your life span was seventy years but you never aged?	Why might a nonsmoker take up smoking?	How might your fitness and/or diet change in the future?
Imagination	What could happen if there were no advertising campaigns for junk food?	Where might we exercise in the future? Why?	What might happen if healthy food became twice as expensive as unhealthy food?	What if people could choose the physical and mental attributes of their children before birth?	Why might the government fund healthy school lunches?	How might our thinking about health change in the future? Why?

Name: _____ Date: _____

Focus: _____

Write an activity for one of the columns in each row. Choose three activities.

	Event	Situation	Choice	Person	Reason	Means
Present						
Past						
Possibility						
Probability						
Prediction						
Imagination						

Inquiry

Focus: What makes your community special?

Your mission is to locate resources to investigate the question. Use your best detective skills, and don't forget to note all the details of each resource once you have discovered it.

Places

Where could you go to find out more about your local community? List two places.

People

Who could you interview to find out more about your community? List two people and their contact details.

Books/Magazines

What could you read to find out more about your local community? List three publications.

Websites

How could the internet help you find out about your community? List two useful websites.

Artworks

What artworks have been created to represent your community? List two pieces of art, from the past or present.

Other

Locate one other resource that could be useful in helping you discover what makes your community special.

Select the best three resources for your investigation. Then conduct your investigation!

1 _____because_____

2 _____because_____

3 _____because_____

Resource detective

Name: _____ Date: _____

Focus: _____

Your mission is to locate resources to investigate the question. Use your best detective skills, and don't forget to note all the details of each resource once you have discovered it.

Places
Where could you go to find out? List two places.

People
Who could you interview? List two people and include contact details for them.

Books/Magazines
What could you read to find out more? List three publications.

Websites
How could the internet help you find out more? List two useful websites.

Artworks
What artworks have been created? They might be sculptures, symbols, paintings, photos, cartoons.

Other
Locate one other resource that could be useful in helping you discover more.

Select the best three resources for your investigation. Then conduct your investigation!

1 _____ because _____

2 _____ because _____

3 _____ because _____

Inquiry

Resource detective

I wonder...

Focus: How has the UK changed?

Research the topics about the UK's history. Then pick two different ways to present your work.

- What people have done in the past has influenced the way we live in the UK now.
- People from many cultures have contributed to the UK's economy and way of life.
- The way the British tackle challenges can make a difference to them and the outcome.

Draw a flow chart
Make a poster/mural
Draw a story map
Draw a cartoon strip
Design an advertisement
Make a mobile
Create a diorama
Draw contrasting images
Paint a picture
Make up a game
Write a play or puppet show
Write a recipe

Write a newspaper report
Write a letter
Create a rap, rhyme or song
Write a poem
Write a reflective journal
  entry
Make up a metaphor
Write a pledge
Make a tape recording
Make a video recording
Design a chat show
  interview

List fascinating facts
Create true/false questions
Write a glossary of new
  words
Create an instruction manual
Make up a 'What am I?' quiz
Design a cause and effect
  wheel
Graph major findings
Define key words or ideas
  using symbols
Create a Venn diagram

Assessment criteria

- included all relevant key points and made connections among them
- considered a range of perspectives
- presented ideas clearly
- worked independently.

Check you can demonstrate the understandings and meet the assessment criteria.

I have chosen to: _____

Student signature _____

Teacher signature _____

Parent signature _____

Focus: _____

Choose topics to research about your focus question. Then choose two different ways to present your work.

- _____

- _____

- _____

Draw a flow chart	Write a play or puppet show	List fascinating facts
Make a poster/mural	Write a recipe	Create true/false questions
Draw a story map	Write a newspaper report	Write a glossary of new words
Draw a cartoon strip	Write a letter	Create an instruction manual
Design an advertisement	Create a rap, rhyme or song	Make up a 'What am I?' quiz
Make a mobile	Write a poem	Design a cause and effect
Create a diorama	Write a reflective journal entry	wheel
Draw contrasting images	Make up a metaphor	Graph major findings
Paint a picture	Write a pledge	Define key words or ideas
Design a chat show interview	Make an audio recording	using symbols
Make up a game	Make a video recording	Create a Venn diagram

Assessment criteria

- included all relevant key points and made connections among them
- considered a range of perspectives
- presented ideas clearly
- worked independently.

Check you can demonstrate the understandings and meet the assessment criteria.

I have chosen to: _____

Student signature _____

Teacher signature _____

Parent signature _____

Inquiry

Voices of the people

Focus: What does it mean to take on a challenge?

Research this topic by interviewing people, and gathering and recording what you hear. Seek permission to record what people say.

What will I ask?

Decide on your interview questions. Here are some suggestions. Write two more.

- How would you define 'a challenge'?
- What is something you find challenging to do?
- What was challenging for you when you were my age?
- What are some of the ways you deal with challenges?
- What is a challenge you might have in the future?

- _____

- _____

Who will I ask?

Choose three people to interview. Here are some ideas: a grandparent; a teacher; a teenager; someone from another culture; a shopkeeper; a sportsperson.

I have chosen to interview:

_____because_____

_____because_____

_____because_____

How will you record your interview?

write ☐   audio record ☐   video ☐   other ☐

Sentence starters to reflect on your learning

The most interesting thing I heard was …   This made me think differently about …

I was surprised to hear …   I wish I had asked …

My best question was …   My poorest question was …

Next time I do an interview I will …

Focus: _____

Research this topic by interviewing people, and gathering and recording what you hear. Seek permission to record what people say.

What will I ask?

Write your interview questions.

- _____
- _____
- _____
- _____
- _____
- _____

Who will I ask?

Choose three people to interview. Here are some ideas: a grandparent; a teacher; a teenager; someone from another culture; a shopkeeper; a sportsperson.

I have chosen to interview:

_____because_____

_____because_____

_____because_____

How will you record your interview?

write ☐   audio record ☐   video ☐   other ☐

Sentence starters to reflect on your learning

The most interesting thing I heard was …   This made me think differently about …

I was surprised to hear …   I wish I had asked …

My best question was …   My poorest question was …

Next time I do an interview I will …

Inquiry

Voices of the people

wonder…

Inquiry

Focus: How do animals survive in their environment?

Think of an animal. Show what you already know about how this animal survives on a spider diagram.

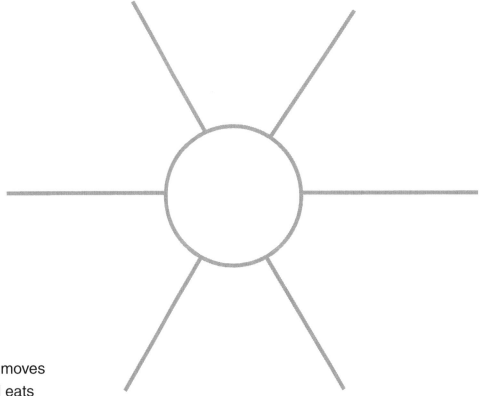

I **must** find out:

- how the animal moves
- what the animal eats
- where the animal lives
- how the animal protects itself.

I **can** find out other interesting things. I would also like to find out: _____

_____

I **will** find out by using:

books ☐   people ☐   TV/DVDs ☐   internet ☐   pictures ☐

I am going to show my thinking and learning by:

writing a book ☐   giving a talk ☐   painting a picture ☐

Must do, can do

Name: _____ Date: _____

Focus: _____

Show what you already know about your topic on a spider diagram.

I **must** find out:

- _____
- _____
- _____
- _____

I **can** find out other interesting things. I would also like to find out:

_____

I will find out by using:

books ☐   people ☐   TV/DVDs ☐   internet ☐   pictures ☐

I am going to show my thinking and learning by:

writing a book ☐   giving a talk ☐   painting a picture ☐

Inquiry

My passion project

My questions

* _____

* _____

* _____

* _____

My goals

* _____

* _____

* _____

* _____

Teacher questions

* _____

* _____

* _____

* _____

Teacher tasks (must do)

* _____

* _____

* _____

* _____

Name: _____   Date: _____

How will I find out?

talk to people ☐

read books ☐

use the internet ☐

go somewhere ☐

watch DVDs ☐

other ☐

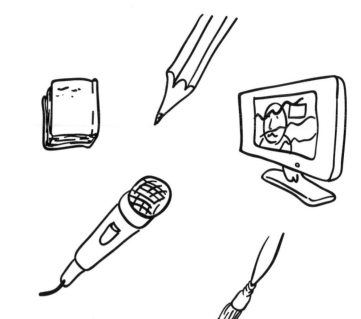

How will I show what I learnt?

draw/paint ☐

write ☐

talk ☐

act ☐

computer presentation ☐

write and present music/song ☐

make something ☐

other ☐

My learning journal

Your notes might include: What have you done? What you are doing? What's next? What are the challenges? How will you tackle them?

Date	Reflections

Quick check ✓ or ✗

- Have I answered the question/s?   Me ☐   Teacher ☐

- Have I completed the teacher tasks?   Me ☐   Teacher ☐

- Have I checked spelling?   Me ☐   Teacher ☐

- Have I completed the learning journal?   Me ☐   Teacher ☐

What I have learnt

About the way I work: _____

_____

_____

_____

_____

About the topic: _____

_____

_____

_____

_____

How well did I do? ★

	My star rating	My comments
Stuck at it		
Worked with others		
Tried hard		
Been neat and tidy		

Teacher comment:

_____

_____

Inquiry

My passion project

Go for goals! – Independent learning tasks

Task	Focus/Area	Brief description	Level
Challenge climb page 86	*How can we form **respectful relationships**?* *Health & wellbeing*	Students work through a sequence of increasingly sophisticated tasks until they reach the 'top of the ladder'.	Middle / Upper
Targetted learning page 88	*How can I keep **myself healthy**?* *Health & wellbeing*	Using a points system and the concept of reaching a 'target', students select various tasks that help explore a particular topic. They then self-assess their efforts.	Upper
Personal, local, global page 90	*How can we use **water** more wisely?* *Society & environment*	Students think about a topic as it relates to them personally. The questions become more challenging as they move from personal to global.	Middle / Upper
A self-assessment matrix page 92	*What makes a **good leader**?* *Society & environment*	Students are encouraged to self-assess their understandings at the end of a unit of work and provide evidence of this understanding. The understanding goals are presented as a sequence from simple to more complex and students rate themselves as beginner, novice or master in relation to each one.	Upper
Think, plan, do page 94	*How can I make a toy with **moving parts**?* *Science & technology*	Students plan a creative or action-oriented project/task. By outlining each step of the planning process, students think through how they will tackle the challenges *before* they actually begin construction or action.	Middle / Upper
Personal best project page 96		These pages could accompany various types of tasks, short and long term. It provides space for students to record their goals, action plan and self-assessment. Cues are provided to support the student in the planning and reflection process.	Middle / Upper

Support materials for independent learning tasks with a focus on personal challenge: 3 Record of conversations with and observations of students; 8 Ideas for developing independent activities; 21 What kind of learner have I been today?; 22 Managing your time checklist; 25 Head, hand and heart self-assessment.

Chapter 5

Go for goals!
A focus on goal setting and personal challenges

The emphasis of the following learning tasks is on personal goal setting and self-improvement, encouraging students to challenge themselves rather than seeing themselves in competition with others. The capacity to set goals and work towards them is a critical aspect of becoming a successful life-long learner. Indeed, in order to be a truly independent, self-managing learner, students must develop the skills and qualities that both enable and inspire them to continue to improve and expand their learning throughout their lives. When we involve students in setting and working towards personal goals, we help develop the understanding that the decisions they make *now* affect them in both the short and long term future.

Tasks that encourage goal setting help focus and energise the learner. Working towards challenging but manageable goals teaches students about the need for persistence and risk taking. Importantly, we also develop in students the vital knowledge that they have some *control* over what they become; that learning is something *they* do, not something done to them!

When students set, work towards and reflect on goals, and when they challenge themselves to improve, they come to understand that:

- when we take **risks** in our learning, we are often **rewarded** by improvement
- we can take **responsibility** for our decisions and actions
- we can always improve what we do and how we do it – we are **continuously evolving**
- **everything we do**, every action we take, may affect the goals we are working towards either positively or negatively
- improvement involves **self-discipline** and **hard work**
- **practice** makes a difference
- we don't always achieve what we think or hope we will but we can **learn from our mistakes**
- success involves **action** – saying what you want to be or do is one thing but it is the action that makes the difference
- **feedback** and **constructive criticism** help us improve ourselves

- goal setting should be an ongoing endeavour – we can set a goal to be achieved in the space of a lesson, a day, a week, a term, a year – and it is more effective when it is a **regular, routine part of classroom life** (and life beyond the classroom)
- **reflection** is an important part of both formulating and working towards goals.

Tips for the classroom

These learning tasks will be easier for students to complete within a classroom context where goal setting and action plans are part of the programme. In developing a classroom programme that includes goal setting, the following tips help ensure success.

Keep the focus clear and narrow

When goals are too broad, they become difficult to plan towards and their success difficult to measure. The more focused the goal, the greater the likelihood that it will be achieved. For example, a goal such as 'to be more organised' lacks clarity and precision. Alternatively, a goal such as 'to complete my homework by and before the due dates' is clear and focused.

Help students be realistic about what they can achieve

Some of the goals students set for themselves are more of a fantasy than a reality! The teacher has a very important role in this regard. Through careful questioning, we need to encourage students to make realistic goals that can be achieved in the time available. Repeated failure to achieve goals will quickly lead to low motivation.

Aim for improvement

While some students set unrealistic goals, others fail to challenge themselves sufficiently, preferring to stay in the 'comfort zone' in order to 'get it right'. Again, the role of the teacher is to advise the student when they think this is happening and to challenge the student to take risks and work towards improvement. Teaching students how to reflect and self-assess can help them set realistic goals. Teacher feedback is also critical in assisting students to identify areas of improvement. We cannot expect students to 'instinctively' understand their needs as learners – it is the teacher's role to support them with clear and specific feedback.

Make a plan!

Setting a goal is one thing but it is the action that one puts into place to achieve the goal that is the most important thing. Once students have identified what they will work on or work towards, they need to plan *how* they will attempt to reach their goal. Many of the structures in this chapter provide support for students in action planning.

Maintain support

While the tasks in this chapter are about individual students setting and working towards goals and challenges, most students will benefit from having some kind of support from fellow students. Students working on similar goals should be encouraged to share their plans and progress with each other. Peer feedback and advice can be a powerful motivator in the process.

Show students how to reward themselves

Encourage students to reward themselves both during and at the end of the process of working towards a goal. Creating a class goal with a planned, shared reward when it is achieved (such as a class excursion or a special lunch) will clearly demonstrate to students the power of incentive as well as the satisfaction of achievement.

Make teaching and learning intentions explicit

It is difficult to set a goal for yourself if you are unclear about the expectations required of a particular task or unit of work. Share your teaching intentions with the students, display and discuss what your hopes are for them, what you want them to come to understand, know and be. Talk with them about how you intend to support them in moving towards those collective goals. This explicit discourse provides a powerful model for students.

Review, reflect and refine

Many goals and the action plans that go with them need to be revised once the process has begun. Encourage students to regularly 'stop and think' about how they are working towards their goals. Journals and log books are useful tools to track and reflect on the process.

Focus: How can we form respectful relationships?

Start at the bottom and work your way up the ladder.

Six points ****

What would help people have more respectful relationships? Create an advertisement that might inform and persuade people.

You made it! Congratulations!

Five points ***

Create a slogan or logo that shows you understand what it takes to have a respectful relationship.

Nearly there ...

Four points **

Create a freeze frame with others, showing what a respectful relationship looks like. Take a digital photo and include labels or speech balloons.

More than half way.

Three points *

Use a Venn diagram to compare and contrast how you might respect yourself and respect someone else.

Keep going!

Two points **

Draw two situations. One that shows a respectful relationship and one that does not.

You've made a start.

One point *

List one way to show a respectful relationship with yourself, others or the environment.

Step up.

Personal challenges

Challenge climb

Name: _____   Date: _____

Focus: _____

Write activities about your topic. Start at the bottom and work your way up the ladder!

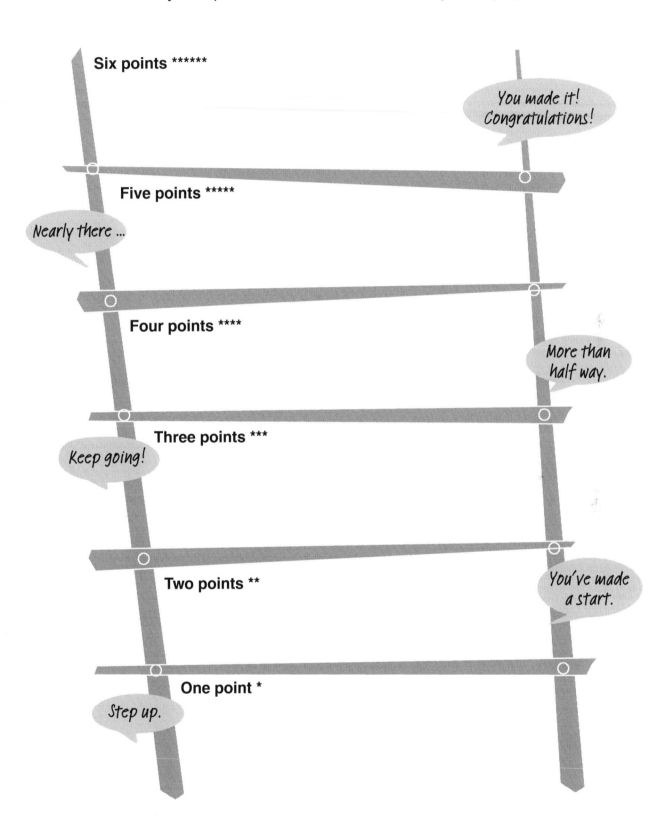

Six points ******

You made it! Congratulations!

Five points *****

Nearly there ...

Four points ****

More than half way.

Three points ***

Keep going!

Two points **

You've made a start.

One point *

Step up.

Name:

Date:

Focus: How can I keep myself healthy?

Decide how many points you would like to earn. Now earn your points!

My total was:

_____ points!

Interview others about what they do to stay healthy. Compare and contrast the information.

Conduct a survey of students' TV viewing habits. What does the survey tell you?

Use a T-chart to compare healthy and unhealthy decisions.

Write the healthy things you do every day.

Create an advertisement that promotes fitness or good nutrition.

5 points

How does food affect our health? Show using a diagram.

Write an exercise plan for one week.

10 points

10 points

20 points

Make a bookmark with 10 healthy hints listed on it.

Create a healthy food scale for the food sold at the canteen.

20 points

Design a brochure for a new health regime.

Draw yourself doing healthy things.

How does one healthy choice lead to others? Use a flow chart or consequence wheel.

List five things you can do to stay healthy.

Design a fitness circuit for your age group.

Find five resources that are about keeping healthy. Order them from most to least interesting and explain your choices.

I achieved my target because …

I did not achieve my target because …

Next time I need to …

Name: _____ Date: _____

Focus: _____

Write activities. Earn your points!

My total was:

_____ points!

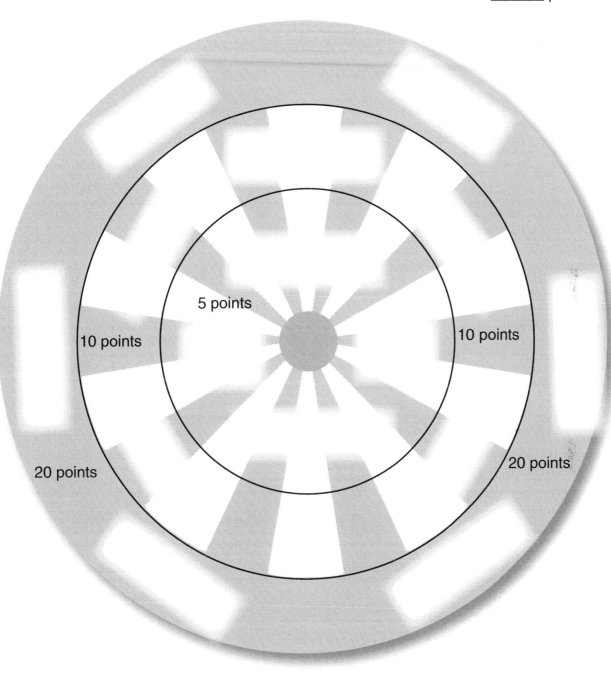

5 points

10 points

10 points

20 points

20 points

I achieved my target because …

I did not achieve my target because …

Next time I need to …

Name: _____   Date: _____

Focus: How can we use water more wisely?

Step **up** from personal to global.

Global community

What should we do as a global community to ensure our water is available for future generations?

_____

_____

Country

What is one thing we should do as a country to conserve our water?

_____

_____

Neighbourhood

What is one way your neighbourhood could be more 'waterwise'?

_____

_____

Friends

What could you and your friends do together to avoid wasting water?

_____

_____

Family

What is something your family could do to reduce the amount of water you use each day?

_____

_____

Personal

What is one thing you can do to use water more wisely?

_____

_____

Reflection

The easiest thing to put into action would be _____

because_____

The most challenging thing to put into action would be _____

because _____

© J Wilson & K Murdoch 2009 **Learning for Themselves** Routledge

Name: _____   **Date:** _____

Focus: _____

Step **up** from personal to global.

Global community

What should we do as   _____
a global community to
                             _____

Country

What is one thing we   _____
should do as a country to
                             _____

Neighbourhood

What is one way your   _____
neighbourhood could
                             _____

Friends

What could you and   _____
your friends do to
                             _____

Family

What is something your   _____
family could do to
                             _____

Personal

What is one thing you   _____
can do to
                             _____

Reflection

The easiest thing to put into action would be _____

because_____

The most challenging thing to put into action would be _____

because _____

Personal challenges

A self-assessment matrix

Focus: What makes a good leader?

Read the statements about leadership. Tick your level of understanding (beginner, novice or master) and give some examples to show your understanding of the statement.

	Beginner: Still on the diving board	Novice: Shallow end	Master! Deep end	Evidence of my understanding (examples)
Basic understanding There are many different kinds of leaders.				
The next step In our community, there are qualities commonly associated with good leaders.				
Extend yourself There are ways each one of us can develop our potential for leadership in different aspects of our lives.				
A challenge! People have different views of what makes a good leader. These views are influenced by many factors including cultural background, time in history and prior experiences.				

Which statements would you now like to find out more about?

How could you investigate these ideas further?

Name: _____ Date: _____

Focus: _____

Think about the topic. Write statements to show different levels of understanding. Tick your level of understanding (beginner, novice, master) and give examples to show your understanding of the statement.

	Beginner: Still on the diving board	Novice: Shallow end	Master! Deep end	Evidence of my understanding (examples)
Basic understanding				
The next step				
Extend yourself				
A challenge!				

Focus: How can I make a toy with moving parts?

Step 1: Visualise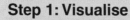

What will it look like?

Imagine what your toy will look like when complete. Draw a picture to show your ideas.

Step 2: Justify ②

Why will this be a good toy?

List why you think this would make a good toy. Try to come up with at least three reasons.

Step 3: Seek advice ③

What did they say?

Now check with two others (including your teacher).

Step 4: Analyse ④

What will I need? Where will I get them? What do I need to do?

Think about what materials you will need, where you will get the materials, and what you will need to do to get the job done.

Step 5: Trouble shoot ⑤

What if ... ?

What might get in the way of making this toy the way you want to? What could go wrong? How will you avoid these things?

Step 6: Inform yourself ⑥

What do I need to find out?

Think if you need to find out anything or if you are not sure about something.

Step 7: Connect ⑦

Who can help?

List the people that might help you make your toy or help you as you work.

Step 8: Plan ⑧

When will I do what I have to do?

Make a timeline of what you need to do now and when you will do it.

Step 9: Reward ⑨

Well done!

What will you do to reward yourself when you have finished the toy?

Personal challenges

Think, plan, do

Name: _____   Date: _____

Focus: _____

1

Step 1: Visualise
What will it look like?

2

Step 2: Justify
Why will this be a good idea?

9

Step 9: Reward
Well done!

3

Step 3: Seek advice
What did they say?

8

Step 8: Plan
When will I do what I have to do?

7

Step 7: Connect
Who can help?

4

Step 4: Analyse
What will I need? Where will I get them?
What do I need to do?

6

Step 6: Inform yourself
What do I need to find out?

5

Step 5: Trouble shoot
What if ... ?

Name: _____ Date: _____

Focus: _____

This is your chance to do your best on a project of your choice. To get started, think of your goals, a plan of action and then how you will assess your work. Have fun!

Ideas for goal setting

Creative communication of ideas

Working with others

Planning

Showing links between ideas

Trying new strategies

Presenting work clearly

Meeting timelines

Organising work

My goals

_____
_____
_____

My action plan

_____
_____

I will know I've done my best if I have:

_____
_____

Teacher comment

_____

Reflection

Use these questions to help you with your reflection.

Did I meet my goals?

Goal 1: Yes ☐ No ☐   Goal 2: Yes ☐ No ☐   Goal 3: Yes ☐ No ☐

What helped or hindered me?

_____

What was the most challenging part?

_____

What am I proud of?

_____

How would I rate my effort?

_____

How do I feel about my work?

_____

Did I self-assess or seek feedback from others as I worked?

_____

What did I learn?

_____

What do I need to improve?

_____

Teacher comment

_____

_____

Bibliography

Blythe, T and Associates 1998, *The Teaching for Understanding Guide*, Jossey Bass, San Francisco.

Bruner, JS 1966, *Toward a Theory of Instruction*, Belknap, Cambridge.

Butler, K 1993, *Connections: Learning Styles of Thinking and Multiple Intelligences*, The Learners Dimension, Columbia, CT.

Coil, C 1999, *Teacher's Toolbox: Integrating Instruction and Units*, Hawker Brownlow, Moorabbin.

Costa, A and Kallick, B (eds) 2000, *Habits of Mind*, ASCD, Alexandria, VA.

De Bono, E 1992, *Six Thinking Hats*, Hawker Brownlow, Moorabbin.

Dewey, J 1938, *Experience and Education*, Collier Books, New York (Collier edition first published 1963)

Edwards, J 1999, *Learning and the Teaching of Thinking: Implications for Gifted Education*, Incorporated Association of Registered Teachers of Victoria, Seminar series number 8.

Gardner, H 1983, *Frames of Mind: The Theory of Multiple Intelligences*, Basic Books, New York.

Glasser, W 1998, *The Quality School Teacher*, Harper Collins, New York.

Godinho, S and Wilson, J 2004, *How to Succeed with Questioning*, Curriculum Corporation, Melbourne.

Gregorc, A *The Gregorc Style Delineator*, Gregorc Associates, Columbia, CT.

Jensen, E 1998, *Super Teaching (Third Edition)*, Focus Education Australia, Flagstaff Hill, South Australia.

Murdoch, K & Wilson, J 2004, *Learning Links: Strategic Teaching for the Learner-Centred Classroom*, Curriculum Corporation, Melbourne.

Murdoch, K 1998, *Classroom Connections*, Eleanor Curtain, Melbourne.

Pohl, M 2002, *Infusing Thinking into the Middle Years*, Hawker Brownlow Education, Moorabbin.

Pohl, M 2000, *Learning to Think, Thinking to Learn*, Hawker Brownlow, Moorabbin.

Pohl, M 1997, *Teaching Thinking Skills in the Primary Years*, Hawker Brownlow, Moorabbin.

Ritchhart, R 2002, *Intellectual Character: What It Is, Why It Matters, and How to Get It*, Jossey Bass, San Francisco.

Taylor, J 1991, *Notes on an Unhurried Journey*, Four Walls, Eight Windows Publishing, New York.

Wilson, J and Cutting, L 2004, *How to Succeed with Contracts*, Curriculum Corporation, Melbourne.

Wilson, J and Wing Jan, L 2007, *Smart Thinking*, Curriculum Corporation, Melbourne.

Wilson, J and Wing Jan, L 2003, *Focus on Inquiry*, Curriculum Corporation, Melbourne.

Websites

Tony Ryan website: Thinker's keys
> http://www.tonyryan.com.au/cms/pages/!/display.html

Project Zero website: Thinking gears
> http://www.pz.harvard.edu/

Organising for independence: Support materials

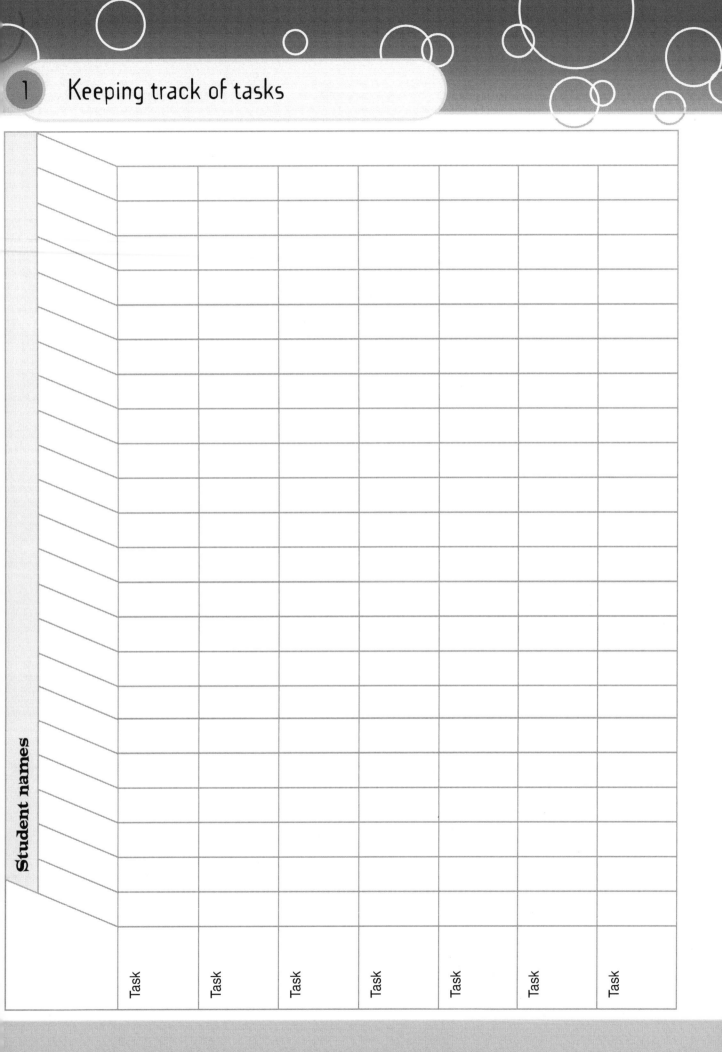

Student names

Task

Task

Task

Task

Task

Task

Task

Name	Has completed plan/proposal	Has identified learning goals	Has collected and synthesised data	Has communicated learning to others	Has reflected on learning

Follow up required:

Name	Date	Notes/observations	Future action needed

4 My weekly diary

Day	Tasks	✓ Completed	To do next week
Monday			
Tuesday			
Wednesday			
Thursday			
Friday			

Name: Date:

5 My individual record sheet

Activity	Date started	Date finished	Comments and reflections

Puzzles

Construction

Reading

Dress ups

Drawing

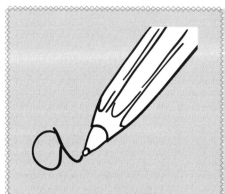

Writing

Play dough

Listening post

Puppets

Cars

Sand and animals

Free choice

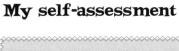

6   Free choice tickets record sheet

Paste your choice on this record sheet. Colour a face.

My choice   **My self-assessment**

I have done: **I felt:**

I have done: **I felt:**

I have done: **I felt:**

I have done: **I felt:**

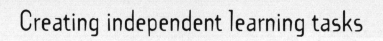

7 Creating independent learning tasks

Planning facets	Examples and questions
1 Curriculum context Consider the **curriculum context** and conceptual ideas (if applicable) in which the task is located: literacy, the arts, science or cross curricula content, and so on.	Identity, interdependence, relationships, adaptation, wellbeing, change, diversity, power
2 Teaching focus Decide what your major **teaching focus** is: knowledge, skills, dispositions, behaviours.	Critical literacy, data collection, group work, confidence, self-management
3 Learning framework Select a **learning framework** and a **presentation layout** that best suits your purposes and those of your students. Many example frameworks have been provided in this book. The use of a range of frameworks across the year is suggested.	Multiple intelligences, learning modalities, learning styles, passion projects, inquiry planner, tic tac toe, pick-a-box, personal best projects
4 Design the activities At task commencement, consider the following: presentation, expectations, grouping, organisation, time frame available, assessment and record keeping, student choices/responsibilities. (See proformas 8, 9 and 10 for ideas. Students could be involved in making these decisions.)	When will students be asked to: work as a whole class, in small groups, across grades, individually? What parts of the requirements will be wholly negotiated? What parts partially negotiated?
5 Record keeping Choose **record keeping** routines that suit the assessment requirements.	Interpersonal, thinking skills, dispositions, knowledge

Design

Model/diorama

Kidspiration/other software

Advertisement

Animation

Invent

A new product

Adapt an idea

Using ICT

BAR (Bigger, Add, Remove)

Imagine

Write a letter

You are/could …

Visualise and draw

Puppet play

Analyse and synthesise

Rap/jingle

Slogan/motto

Bundling

Logo

Classify

Cluster web

Concept map

Reverse key

Mind map

Compare

Venn diagram

Data chart

T-chart

Continuum

Sequence

Storymap/ladder

Comic strip

Cycle map

Write a manual or a wiki

Critique

PMI

SWOT (Strengths, Weaknesses, Opportunities Threats)

Recipe

Create a chat show

Predict

What if …?

Key words and images

Brainstorm

What is likely, unlikely, impossible?

Rank/prioritise

Conduct a vote

Survey and graph

Diamond ranking

List in priority order

Cause and effect

Fishbone

Bridge

Futures wheel

Flowchart

Question

The answer is … what's the question?

Q matrix

Socratic/divergent questions

Self-question

Evaluate

Use scales to show …

Position paper

ECG

Criteria/checklist

Present awards

Perspectives

Court case/debate

De Bono's hats

Moral dilemma

Draw/find four contrasting images

Reflect

Mind map

Journal

Reflective cue cards

Personal pledge

Metaphors/quotes

Sensory activities	Dramatic play	Creation centre	Writing	Reading/ research
Shells	Dress ups, for example hats, masks, bags, glasses	Plasticine	Ready-made diaries	Books
Sandpaper and blocks		Play dough	Letter writing materials	Magazines
Sand	Jewellery	Boxes	Different size paper	Menus
Musical instruments	Food boxes	Tape		Pamphlets/ brochures
Needle and thread	Saucepans	Pipe cleaners	Different pens, textas, crayons, charcoal, paints	Photos
Puzzles	Stove	Unifix		Cartoons
Cooking ingredients and equipment	Cash register	Mobilo		Maps
	Large boxes, for example fridge	Feathers		Atlas
Water/rice and measuring jugs	Juggling balls	Buttons	Old typewriter	Recipe books
Velvet and different kinds of fabrics	Play phone, fax, computer	Beads	Plastic letters	Labelled diagrams
		Coloured paper	Magnetic letters	Dictionary
Locks and keys	Pegs, clothesline	Stamps		Telephone books
Magnifying glass	Tools and wood	Scissors	Small chalk boards and chalk	Guides
Kaleidoscopes	Maps	Balloons		Internet
Dough/clay	Tickets	Feathers	Stapler	Newspapers
Paper and paste	Invitations	Cupcake pans	Hole punch	Calendar
Felt board	Tea sets	Balloons	Tape	Posters
Rice/dried beans	Puppets	Bubble wrap	Sticky tape	Video/audio tapes
Pebbles/small stones	Dolls	Confetti	Stamps	Song books
Mirrors	Soft toys	Clay	Envelopes	Listening post
Prisms	Shoes	Stamp and stamp pads	Post-it notes	Globe
Magnets	Musical instruments	Paper and paste	Highlighter pens	Art books
	Magic wand	Stickers	Computer	Business cards
		Foil	Paper clips	Thesaurus
		String		

VISUAL

- Design pictorial symbols
- Conduct a media search
- Make daily observation records-chart or graph
- Write a letter
- Create a timeline
- Make a glossary of key words
- Draw a story map
- Research relevant statistics and find patterns
- Do a book/CD/web search
- Draw a cartoon strip
- Create a concept/mind map
- Retell as a cartoon using speech bubbles
- Retell events as a board game
- Create events/consequence chart/tree
- Rewrite as a folktale, fable, fairytale, myth, legend
- Paint/draw three key pictures
- Collect quotes to describe/prove or disprove
- Write or select poetry to describe feelings/ findings
- Use a slide show to summarise key ideas
- Graph information
- Start a reflective journal
- Create a visual organiser, for example, data chart, fish bone, flow chart, graph or map, T-chart or Y-chart, PMI chart, Venn diagram
- Draw a poster or collage
- Paint a mural
- Write a catchy newspaper heading or article
- Create a wiki or blog
- Produce a digital story
- Use Kidspiration or Inspiration to visually represent your ideas
- Design a promotion brochure
- Write a blurb
- Make a big/little fact book
- Write a play
- Write the questions/responses for a talk show
- Design a word find or crossword
- Write a list or manual of instructions/ directions
- Make up a test or true/false quiz questions
- Write who/what am I? quiz questions
- Take some photos and attach captions
- Use PowerPoint or another computer program to prepare a presentation
- Make a 'wanted' poster
- Design a medal or certificate
- Draw four contrasting images
- Write a report for the school, local or other newspaper or magazine
- Write a personal pledge
- Design and present an advertisement or banner
- Create metaphors to explain your ideas
- Write a position paper
- Make a list of summary statements
- Write a recipe, formula, balanced diet, menu
- Write a fable or legend
- Use the thinking hats to structure writing or images
- Make a photo album
- Design a banner, badge, slogan, motto or logo
- Create criteria to judge items/information
- Collect magazine pictures or use images from clip art to represent your ideas

AUDITORY

- Recite a monologue
- Make an audiotape
- Form a hypothesis and check against others
- Design and conduct a questionnaire
- Conduct a peer teaching session
- Present both sides of an argument as a court case
- Explain a personal philosophy
- Retell using music and movement
- Make phone calls to seek information
- Talk to others about your ideas and questions
- Write a song or chant
- Discuss ideas using SWOT (Strengths, Weaknesses, Opportunities and Threats)
- Make up a song or rap
- Create a soundscape
- Make an audio or videotape
- Make a radio commercial
- Conduct a vote/referendum
- Engage in a debate
- Conduct a chat show or current affairs show
- Present the results of a committee review
- Compare to see if you have things in common with…
- Write and read an acrostic poem
- Recite a created limerick
- Make sound effects
- Create a proverb or riddle
- Do some future gazing
- Narrate a story
- Find or write a song that explains an idea
- Search for pieces of music that explain your ideas
- Use a known song/melody and write new words
- Make a pod cast
- Use the computer to record a rap or poem

KINESTHETIC

- Create sculpture
- Play charades
- Make a jigsaw from your findings including all the relevant pieces
- Make a pop-up book or card
- Make simple devices/products
- Make a board game, for example like Trivial Pursuit to demonstrate your new knowledge
- Use construction materials or play dough to make a model
- Make a diorama
- Make a mobile
- Sew a patchwork quilt or tapestry
- Make shadow/stick/finger puppets to dramatise
- Make a frieze
- Write and enact a role-play
- Design and create tests or experiments to collect information
- Put on a puppet performance
- Create and present awards
- Set up a living exhibition of your learning
- Present a television documentary
- Show main ideas through freeze frame or skits
- Find objects to represent your ideas
- Use your body to make symbols that express your ideas
- Create a dance sequence to express your ideas
- Use 'found objects' to tell a story/explain something
- Create a treasure hunt

Name: _____   Date: _____

Planning and getting ready	
Focus	What do I already know?
	What interests me?
	What do I want to know about? (personal, physical, social world works)
	Why is this important to me?
Pose questions	What is challenging but achievable in the time allowed?
	How will knowing this contribute to my life or the life of others?
Set goals and timelines	What skills, work and mind habits could I practise?
	How will I know if this has been a successful investigation?
	What evidence can I collect to show what I have
Set criteria for success	★ learned about?
	★ learned to do?
	★ learned about learning?

Seeking and sorting information	
Gather a range of information	Where will I find relevant information?
	What are the key ideas?
	How will I know if this information is useful or accurate?
	Have I considered different points of view?
Sort	How will I organise and summarise the information?
	What connections can I make among big ideas?
	How can I clearly show these connections?
Share and show others	What have I learned that is important to share with others? Why?
	How can I best share my learning?
	Who is the audience and what are their needs?
	What can I do to engage my audience?

Reflecting, forward planning and action	
Reflect on:	What do I now know?
★ learning	What can I do that I couldn't before?
★ knowledge	Have I answered my questions?
★ the way you have worked	Have I reached my goals?
	What have I learnt about my learning that I can improve/change next time?
Apply learning	What do I need to do now?
	What will I do with what I have learnt?
	How can I use this to inform/help others?

12 My contract

I_____

agree to complete the following work to the best of my ability and

submit it by the due date: _____

* Complete_____ activities

Activities:_____

* _____

* _____

* _____

Attend a conference

Date:_____

_____

_____

_____

Signed: _____ (student) Date: _____

Signed: _____ (parent) Date: _____

Signed: _____ (teacher) Date: _____

13 My contract planner

Non-negotiable tasks

Completion dates

- _____ _____

- _____ _____

- _____ _____

Negotiable

Student led expert groups

- _____ _____

- _____ _____

- _____ _____

Teacher led workshops

- _____ _____

- _____ _____

- _____ _____

Independent tasks

- _____ _____

- _____ _____

- _____ _____

- _____ _____

- _____ _____

- _____ _____

Name: _____ Date: _____

14 Planning and reflecting

Thinking ahead → Timelines

Completion date: _____

Teacher check-ins

Comments: _____

_____ Date: _____

Comments: _____

_____ Date: _____

Questions to think about

What do I already know?   What are the possible ways to get this task done?

What do I want or need to learn about?   What materials do I need?

How will I find out what I need to know?   What are my goals?

Why is this important?   What is my plan of action?

_____

_____

Thinking back ← Thinking about learning and the way I worked

Did I focus on my work?   Did I encourage others?   Did I share ideas?

Did I give feedback to others?   Did I use my time effectively?

What can I do that I couldn't before?   What did I learn?

What have I learnt about my learning that I can improve or change next time?

_____

_____

Questions before presenting and submitting

Is it my best work?   Is it practical?

Does the product satisfy a need or meet my goals?

_____

_____

Peer checker

Comments: _____

_____ Date: _____

15   Group planning sheet

Names of team members

_____

_____

The task is: _____

_____

What resources are needed?

* _____

* _____

* _____

Who will do what?

Name	Role or jobs

Assessment criteria

* _____

* _____

* _____

* _____

16 Presentation planner and assessment sheet

My personal presentation goal is:

_____

_____

_____

My main purpose is to:

☐ express ☐ inform ☐ persuade ☐ entertain ☐ instruct

☐ _____

☐ _____

Presentation type (may be more than one):

☐ poster – painting or drawing ☐ model ☐ drama/role-play ☐ storytelling
☐ digital (for example, PowerPoint) ☐ poetry ☐ song or musical piece

☐ _____

☐ _____

Feedback on goal, purpose and presentation		
Peer assessment	**Self-assessment**	**Teacher assessment**

Teacher auditing checklist

Have I/we created opportunities for students to organise and represent their ideas in different ways?				
For example, will students:	Task	Task	Task	Task
• reflect on and ask questions about their thinking, learning, feelings, and actions?				
• set their own goals?				
• work with others?				
• consider issues from different perspectives?				
• think inductively and deductively?				
• make connections and reason?				
• listen and speak with others?				
• use written and spoken language for a range of purposes?				
• graphically/diagrammatically process and represent ideas?				
• use movement to express and represent ideas and feelings?				
• be involved in hands-on activities?				
• communicate expressively through performance?				

Have I been an independent learner?

I made a plan.	I checked my own work.	I thought about different ways to solve my problem. 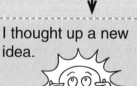	I took some risks beyond my comfort zone. 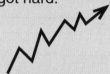
I kept going even when it got hard. 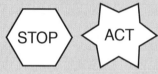	I stopped to think before I acted. 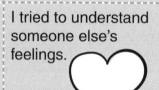	I tried to understand someone else's feelings.	I thought up a new idea.
I asked myself questions.	I made links with what I already know. 	I took time to read over my work. 	I learned something from others. 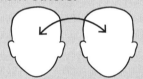
I thought about my thinking.	I was eager and enthusiastic.	I searched and found resources for myself.	I set myself goals and worked towards them. 
I stayed positive even when it was challenging.	I avoided distractions. 	I stayed on task. 	I was organised. 
I tried useful ways to help me get the job done.	I managed my time well.	I tried a new way of doing something.	I sought feedback on my progress. 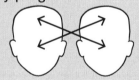
I stopped to think about what I was doing.	I self-assessed.	I changed my way of thinking/working.	I helped others.

What can I do if: **I can't find the information I need?**

- Think about different ways to get the information. For example, talk to people, read books, watch DVDs, search the internet, visit places.
- Ask others where they got information.
- Double check the sources you do have.
- If all else fails, reconsider your focus questions.

What can I do if: **I have lots of information?**

- Sort the information into groups of 'like ideas'.
- Create a data chart or use another visual organiser to organise your information, remembering to note the source of each piece of information.
- Check information with the latest sources and/or experts.
- If you are getting bogged down, take a break, do a simpler task and then come back to it.
- Try to summarise the 'big ideas'. Five key points can later be elaborated with examples, references and details.
- Ask someone else to listen to your summary of the information and ask you questions. This can help you clarify what you know and point out gaps.

What can I do if: **I lose motivation?**

- Think about what you want to achieve and why.
- Break up the task requirements and tackle a bit that is easy to get done.
- Talk to someone about what you have achieved and get their ideas about what to do next.
- Take a moment to relax and give yourself a pat on the back for what you have done.
- List key ideas and questions that you could pursue next.

What can I do if: **I can't get along with my team members?**

- Talk to them first about what you want to achieve and how you feel without blaming anyone.
- Try to see everyone's point of view.
- Focus on the task and share jobs that everyone is happy with.
- Make a point of encouraging and thanking others (and yourself) for their contribution to the tasks.
- Remember that working with others can improve the quality of your work and be more enjoyable than working alone.

Organisation

Hints

- Make a list or draw pictures of all the jobs that need to be done.
- Tick off all the jobs you have completed and feel good about.
- Put the jobs in order of priority and start with the most important.
- Make time to organise the ideas and materials you have before you start and after you have finished a job. Time spent organising is well spent.
- If your organisation techniques haven't worked before, try new ones.

Focus

Hints

- Make time to think of all the jobs that need to be done.
- Eat some brain food, stretch and relax.
- Start working. Once you start the ideas may flow quicker. It doesn't have to be perfect.
- Talk to others about what you have done and are thinking.
- Reread what you have done already to help refocus.
- If all else fails come back to it later!

Running out of time

Hints

- Get started on a small task. You could get on a roll!
- Put aside some uninterrupted thinking and working time and don't let anything distract you.
- Use graphic organisers to summarise what you have done.
- Make a plan to do all the jobs that still need doing.
- Make time to reread your work and have someone else check it for you.

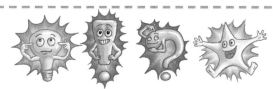

Losing motivation

Hints

- Think about what you want to achieve and why.
- Break up the task requirements and tackle a bit that is easy to get done.
- Talk to someone about what you have achieved and get their ideas about what to do next.
- Take a moment to relax and give yourself a pat on the back for what you have done.
- List key ideas and questions that you could pursue next.

Getting along with a team

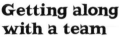

Hints

- Talk to team members first about problems, what you want to achieve and how you feel without blaming anyone.
- Try to see everyone's point of view.
- Focus on the task and share jobs that everyone is happy with.
- Make a point of encouraging and thanking others (and yourself) for their contributions.
- Remember that working with others can improve the quality of your work and can be more enjoyable than working alone.

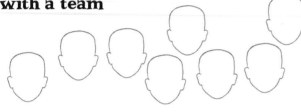

Can't find information

Hints

- Think about different ways to get the information. For example, talk to people, read books, watch DVDs, search the internet, visit places.
- Ask others about where they got information.
- Double check the sources you do have.
- If all else fails, reconsider your focus questions.

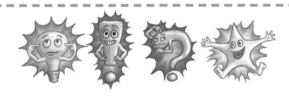

Too much information

Hints

- Sort the information into groups of 'like ideas'.
- Create a data chart or use another visual organiser to organise your information. Remember to note the source of each piece of information.
- Check information with the latest sources and/or experts.
- If you are getting bogged down, take a break and do a simpler task and come back to it.
- Try to summarise the 'big ideas'. Key points can later be elaborated with examples, references and details.
- Ask someone else to listen to your summary of the information and ask you questions. This can help you clarify what you know and point out gaps.

20 Reminders for group work

Before you start working together as a group...

Each group member needs to choose a **personal goal**. ☐

Discuss how the team will complete the task. Write down any **team goals**. ☐

Choose a **checker** who will check that all group tasks are completed. ☐

Choose a **recorder** who will record the discussion. ☐

Consider whether you need to allocate any of the following **roles**:

- timekeeper ☐

- encourager ☐

- observer ☐

- coordinator. ☐

Before you present...

Choose a **reporter** who will record the discussion. ☐

Reflect on your own performance. ☐

If you noticed someone else meeting their goal, give them **feedback**. ☐

The checker should **check** that all task requirements are completed. ☐

If being peer assessed...

Choose the criteria for peer presentation. ☐

Hint: This has to be something the audience can comment on, for example clarity of presentation, ability to answer questions, organisation of main ideas.

Name:

Date:

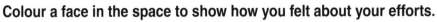

21 What kind of learner have I been today?

Colour a face in the space to show how you felt about your efforts.

Things to think about	Monday	Tuesday	Wednesday	Thursday	Friday
I concentrated.	☺ ☹ ☐	☺ ☹ ☐	☺ ☹ ☐	☺ ☹ ☐	☺ ☹ ☐
I asked good questions.	☺ ☹ ☐	☺ ☹ ☐	☺ ☹ ☐	☺ ☹ ☐	☺ ☹ ☐
I finished my work.	☺ ☹ ☐	☺ ☹ ☐	☺ ☹ ☐	☺ ☹ ☐	☺ ☹ ☐
I shared with others.	☺ ☹ ☐	☺ ☹ ☐	☺ ☹ ☐	☺ ☹ ☐	☺ ☹ ☐
I did lots of thinking.	☺ ☹ ☐	☺ ☹ ☐	☺ ☹ ☐	☺ ☹ ☐	☺ ☹ ☐
I took care of my things.	☺ ☹ ☐	☺ ☹ ☐	☺ ☹ ☐	☺ ☹ ☐	☺ ☹ ☐
I learned something new.	☺ ☹ ☐	☺ ☹ ☐	☺ ☹ ☐	☺ ☹ ☐	☺ ☹ ☐
I helped someone else.	☺ ☹ ☐	☺ ☹ ☐	☺ ☹ ☐	☺ ☹ ☐	☺ ☹ ☐
I felt proud of myself.	☺ ☹ ☐	☺ ☹ ☐	☺ ☹ ☐	☺ ☹ ☐	☺ ☹ ☐

22 Managing your time checklist

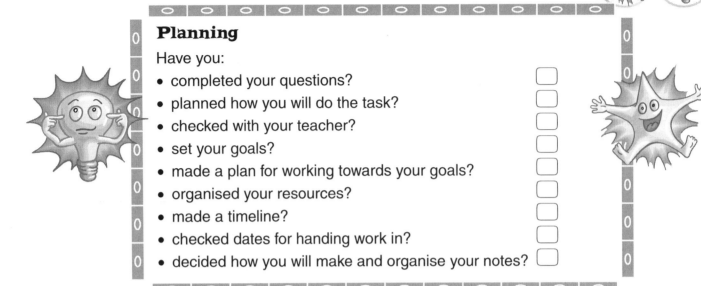

Planning

Have you:

- completed your questions? ☐
- planned how you will do the task? ☐
- checked with your teacher? ☐
- set your goals? ☐
- made a plan for working towards your goals? ☐
- organised your resources? ☐
- made a timeline? ☐
- checked dates for handing work in? ☐
- decided how you will make and organise your notes? ☐

Investigating

Have you:

- contacted people or places you plan to talk to/visit? ☐
- gained permission to use material? ☐
- written down the full reference for any books or websites you have used? ☐
- written the ideas down in your own words? ☐
- used more than one source of information? ☐
- checked where the information is from and whether it is trustworthy? ☐
- compared information from different sources? ☐
- made sure you *understand* what you have read or found out? ☐
- answered all your questions and completed all the tasks? ☐

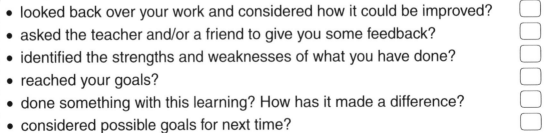

Reflecting and acting

Have you:

- looked back over your work and considered how it could be improved? ☐
- asked the teacher and/or a friend to give you some feedback? ☐
- identified the strengths and weaknesses of what you have done? ☐
- reached your goals? ☐
- done something with this learning? How has it made a difference? ☐
- considered possible goals for next time? ☐

23 My learning journal

You could include:

- what you did
- any challenges and how you tackled them
- whether you worked with others and why
- what you need to do next
- what you are learning
- what help you think you need.

Date	Reflections	Peer, teacher and parent comments

Name: Date:

24 My double entry learning journal

Reflection starters

I wish …   I feel …   I like …

I saw …   I learnt …   Looking back …

It was hard …   I am puzzled …   I could have …

I know …   I can …   I am proud …   What if? …   My question is …   I wonder …

Date	What I did	Reflection

25 Head, hand and heart self-assessment

Head

What did you think about?

What have you learnt?

How would you do it next time?

_____

_____

_____

_____

_____

Hand

What did you do that was handy, helpful or skilful?

_____

_____

_____

_____

_____

Heart

How do you feel about your work?

How do you feel about how you have worked?

_____

_____

_____

_____

Analyse the factors that assisted you to learn this term. What were the most and least useful?	How could you change an aspect of your work to improve it?	*What were your achievements?*
What would be included on your summary of highlights and lowlights?	**What award would you get for your efforts?**	What did you learn about? What did you learn to do?
Compare two different lessons. What did you do that made a difference?	*What is one part of your behaviour that you'd like to minify or magnify?*	**How would you rate your performance?**
Evaluate your overall performance from someone else's viewpoint. How well did you do?	**If you could learn a new skill to help you learn what would it be?**	What do you want to find out more about?
Create a list of your attributes. Which one is the most important?	Draw you at work. If you had extra resources to help you, what would they be?	*How/when will you use something you have learnt again?*
If you continue to work the way you have been, what do you think the results might be?	**Think of many ways to learn differently. Which ones could you try?**	What did someone do or say that made you really think? Why?

27 Self-assessment

Here are some ideas for your reflective comments.

Risk-taking Use of resources Behaviour Thinking

Learning Teamwork Time management Enthusiasm Skills

Perseverance Feelings Organisation

Choices	Reflections

28 Pick-a-box self-assessment

I picked these tasks (colour the numbers).

My favourite was number ⬜

It was my favourite because

_____

_____

_____

_____

I learnt about/to/to be

_____

_____

_____

_____

Teacher comment

_____

_____

_____

_____